SUZUKI
4x4
FOR SERIOUS OFF-ROAD ACTION

Also from Veloce:

Speedpro Series
4-Cylinder Engine Short Block High-Performance Manual – New Updated & Revised Edition (Hammill)
Alfa Romeo DOHC High-performance Manual (Kartalamakis)
Alfa Romeo V6 Engine High-performance Manual (Kartalamakis)
BMC 998cc A-series Engine, How to Power Tune (Hammill)
1275cc A-series High-performance Manual (Hammill)
Camshafts – How to Choose & Time Them For Maximum Power (Hammill)
Competition Car Datalogging Manual, The (Templeman)
Cylinder Heads, How to Build, Modify & Power Tune – Updated & Revised Edition (Burgess & Gollan)
Distributor-type Ignition Systems, How to Build & Power Tune – New 3rd Edition (Hammill)
Fast Road Car, How to Plan and Build – Revised & Updated Colour New Edition (Stapleton)
Ford SOHC 'Pinto' & Sierra Cosworth DOHC Engines, How to Power Tune – Updated & Enlarged Edition (Hammill)
Ford V8, How to Power Tune Small Block Engines (Hammill)
Harley-Davidson Evolution Engines, How to Build & Power Tune (Hammill)
Holley Carburetors, How to Build & Power Tune – Revised & Updated Edition (Hammill)
Honda Civic Type R High-Performance Manual, The (Cowland & Clifford)
Jaguar XK Engines, How to Power Tune – Revised & Updated Colour Edition (Hammill)
Land Rover Discovery, Defender & Range Rover – How to Modify Coil Sprung Models for High Performance & Off-Road Action (Hosier)
MG Midget & Austin-Healey Sprite, How to Power Tune – Enlarged & updated 4th Edition (Stapleton)
MGB 4-cylinder Engine, How to Power Tune (Burgess)
MGB V8 Power, How to Give Your – Third Colour Edition (Williams)
MGB, MGC & MGB V8, How to Improve – New 2nd Edition (Williams)
Mini Engines, How to Power Tune On a Small Budget – Colour Edition (Hammill)
Motorcycle-engined Racing Car, How to Build (Pashley)
Motorsport, Getting Started in (Collins)
Nissan GT-R High-performance Manual, The (Gorodji)
Nitrous Oxide High-performance Manual, The (Langfield)
Race & Trackday Driving Techniques (Hornsey)
Retro or classic car for high performance, How to modify your (Stapleton)
Rover V8 Engines, How to Power Tune (Hammill)
Secrets of Speed – Today's techniques for 4-stroke engine blueprinting & tuning (Swager)
Sportscar & Kitcar Suspension & Brakes, How to Build & Modify – Revised 3rd Edition (Hammill)
SU Carburettor High-performance Manual (Hammill)
Successful Low-Cost Rally Car, How to Build a (Young)
Suzuki 4x4, How to Modify For Serious Off-road Action (Richardson)
Tiger Avon Sportscar, How to Build Your Own – Updated & Revised 2nd Edition (Dudley)
TR2, 3 & TR4, How to Improve (Williams)
TR5, 250 & TR6, How to Improve (Williams)
TR7 & TR8, How to Improve (Williams)
V8 Engine, How to Build a Short Block For High Performance (Hammill)
Volkswagen Beetle Suspension, Brakes & Chassis, How to Modify For High Performance (Hale)
Volkswagen Bus Suspension, Brakes & Chassis for High Performance, How to Modify – Updated & Enlarged New Edition (Hale)
Weber DCOE, & Dellorto DHLA Carburetors, How to Build & Power Tune – 3rd Edition (Hammill)

RAC handbooks
Caring for your car – How to maintain & service your car (Fry)
Caring for your car's bodywork and interior (Nixon)
Caring for your bicycle – How to maintain & repair your bicycle (Henshaw)
Caring for your scooter – How to maintain & service your 49cc to 125cc twist & go scooter (Fry)
Efficient Driver's Handbook, The (Moss)
Electric Cars – The Future is Now! (Linde)
First aid for your car – Your expert guide to common problems & how to fix them (Collins)
How your car works (Linde)
Motorhomes – A first-time-buyer's guide (Fry)
Pass the MoT test! – How to check & prepare your car for the annual MoT test (Paxton)
Selling your car – How to make your car look great and how to sell it fast (Knight)
Simple fixes for your car – How to do small jobs for yourself and save money (Collins)

Enthusiast's Restoration Manual Series
Beginner's Guide to Classic Motorcycle Restoration, The (Burns)
Citroën 2CV, How to Restore (Porter)
Classic Car Bodywork, How to Restore (Thaddeus)
Classic British Car Electrical Systems (Astley)
Classic Car Electrics (Thaddeus)
Classic Cars, How to Paint (Thaddeus)
Jaguar E-type (Crespin)
Reliant Regal, How to Restore (Payne)
Triumph TR2, 3, 3A, 4 & 4A, How to Restore (Williams)
Triumph TR5/250 & 6, How to Restore (Williams)
Triumph TR7/8, How to Restore (Williams)
Triumph Trident T150/T160 & BSA Rocket III, How to Restore (Rooke)
Ultimate Mini Restoration Manual, The (Ayre & Webber)
Volkswagen Beetle, How to Restore (Tyler)
VW Bay Window Bus (Paxton)
Yamaha FS1-E, How to Restore (Watts)

Expert Guides
Land Rover Series I-III – Your expert guide to common problems & how to fix them (Thurman)
MG Midget & A-H Sprite – Your expert guide to common problems & how to fix them (Horler)

Essential Buyer's Guide Series
Alfa Romeo Alfasud – All saloon models from 1971 to 1983 & Sprint models from 1976 to 1989 (Metcalfe)
Alfa Romeo Giulia GT Coupé (Booker)
Alfa Romeo Giulia Spider (Booker)
Audi TT (Davies)
Austin Seven (Barker)
Big Healeys (Trummel)
BMW E21 3 Series (1975-1983) (Cook & Wylie)
BMW E30 3 Series (1981 to 1994) (Hosier)
BMW GS (Henshaw)
BMW X5 (Saunders)
Citroën 2CV (Paxton)
Citroën ID & DS (Heilig)
Cobra Replicas (Ayre)
Corvette C2 Sting Ray 1963-1967 (Falconer)
Choosing, Using & Maintaining Your Electric Bicycle (Henshaw)
Fiat 500 & 600 (Bobbitt)
Ford Capri (Paxton)
Ford Escort Mk1 & Mk2 (Williamson)
Ford Model T – All models 1909 to 1927 (Barker)
Ford Mustang – First Generation 1964 to 1973 (Cook)
Ford Mustang – Fifth generation/ S197 (Cook)
Ford RS Cosworth Sierra & Escort (Williamson)
Harley-Davidson Big Twins (Henshaw)
Hillman Imp – All models of the Hillman Imp, Sunbeam Stiletto, Singer Chamois, Hillman Husky & Commer Imp 1963 to 1976 (Morgan)
Jaguar E-Type 3.8 & 4.2-litre (Crespin)
Jaguar E-type V12 5.3-litre (Crespin)
Jaguar Mark 1 & 2 (All models including Daimler 2.5-litre V8) 1955 to 1969 (Thorley)
Jaguar S-Type – 1999 to 2007 (Thorley)
Jaguar X-Type – 2001 to 2009 (Thorley)
Jaguar XJ-S (Crespin)
Jaguar XJ6, XJ8 & XJR (Thorley)
Jaguar XK 120, 140 & 150 (Thorley)
Jaguar XK8 & XKR (1996-2005) (Thorley)
Jaguar/Daimler XJ 1994-2003 (Crespin)
Jaguar/Daimler XJ40 (Crespin)
Jaguar/Daimler XJ6, XJ12 & Sovereign (Crespin)
Kawasaki Z1 & Z900 (Orritt)
Land Rover Series I, II & IIA (Thurman)
Land Rover Series III (Thurman)
Lotus Seven replicas & Caterham 7: 1973-2013 (Hawkins)
Mazda MX-5 Miata (Mk1 1989-97 & Mk2 98-2001) (Crook)
Mazda RX-8 All models 2003 to 2012 (Parish)
Mercedes Benz Pagoda 230SL, 250SL & 280SL roadsters & coupés (Bass)
Mercedes-Benz 190 All 190 models (W201 series) 1982 to 1993 (Parish)
Mercedes-Benz 280-560SL & SLC (Bass)
Mercedes-Benz SL R129 Series (Parish)
Mercedes-Benz W123 All models 1976 to 1986 (Parish)
Mercedes-Benz W124 – All models 1984-1997 (Zoporowski)
MG Midget & A-H Sprite (Horler)
MG TD, TF & TF1500 (Jones)
MGA 1955-1962 (Crosier)
MGB & MGB GT (Williams)
MGF & MG TF (Hawkins)
Mini (Paxton)
Morris Minor & 1000 (Newell)
New Mini (Collins)
Peugeot 205 GTI (Blackburn)
Porsche 911 (964) (Streather)
Porsche 911 (993) (Streather)
Porsche 911 (996) (Streather)
Porsche 911 (997) Model years 2004 to 2009 (Streather)
Porsche 911 (997) Second generation models 2009 to 2012 (Streather)
Porsche 911 Carrera 3.2 (Streather)
Porsche 911 SC (Streather)
Porsche 924 – All models 1976 to 1988 (Hodgkins)
Porsche 928 (Hemmings)
Porsche 930 Turbo & 911 (930) Turbo (Streather)
Porsche 944 (Higgins)
Porsche 986 Boxster (Streather)
Porsche 987 Boxster & Cayman (Streather)
Rolls-Royce Silver Shadow & Bentley T-Series (Bobbitt)
Subaru Impreza (Hobbs)
Sunbeam Alpine (Barker)
Triumph Herald & Vitesse (Davies)
Triumph Spitfire & GT6 (Baugues)
Triumph Stag (Mort)
Triumph TR6 (Williams)
Triumph TR7 & TR8 (Williams)
Volvo 700/900 Series (Beavis)
VW Beetle (Cservenka & Copping)
VW Bus (Cservenka & Copping)
VW Golf GTI (Cservenka & Copping)

Great Cars
Austin-Healey – A celebration of the fabulous 'Big' Healey (Piggott)
Triumph TR – TR2 to 6: The last of the traditional sports cars (Piggott)

Rally Giants Series
Audi Quattro (Robson)
Austin Healey 100-6 & 3000 (Robson)
Fiat 131 Abarth (Robson)
Ford Escort MkI (Robson)
Ford Escort RS Cosworth & World Rally Car (Robson)
Ford Escort RS1800 (Robson)
Lancia Delta 4WD/Integrale (Robson)
Lancia Stratos (Robson)
Mini Cooper/Mini Cooper S (Robson)
Peugeot 205 T16 (Robson)
Saab 96 & V4 (Robson)
Subaru Impreza (Robson)
Toyota Celica GT4 (Robson)

WSC Giants
Audi R8 (Wagstaff)
Ferrari 312P & 312PB (Collins & McDonough)
Gulf-Mirage 1967 to 1982 (McDonough)
Matra Sports Cars – MS620, 630, 650, 660 & 670 – 1966 to 1974 (McDonough)

General
1½-litre GP Racing 1961-1965 (Whitelock)
AC Two-litre Saloons & Buckland Sportscars (Archibald)
Alfa Romeo 155/156/147 Competition Touring Cars (Collins)
Alfa Romeo Giulia Coupé GT & GTA (Tipler)
Alfa Romeo Montreal – The dream car that came true (Taylor)
Alfa Romeo Montreal – The Essential Companion (Classic Reprint of 500 copies) (Taylor)
Alfa Tipo 33 (McDonough & Collins)
Alpine & Renault – The Development of the Revolutionary Turbo F1 Car 1968 to 1979 (Smith)
Alpine & Renault – The Sports Prototypes 1963 to 1969 (Smith)
Alpine & Renault – The Sports Prototypes 1973 to 1978 (Smith)
Anatomy of the Classic Mini (Huthert & Ely)
Anatomy of the Works Minis (Moylan)
Armstrong-Siddeley (Smith)
Art Deco and British Car Design (Down)
Autodrome (Collins & Ireland)
Autodrome 2 (Collins & Ireland)
Automotive A-Z, Lane's Dictionary of Automotive Terms (Lane)
Automotive Mascots (Kay & Springate)
Bahamas Speed Weeks, The (O'Neil)
Bentley Continental, Corniche and Azure (Bennett)
Bentley MkVI, Rolls-Royce Silver Wraith, Dawn & Cloud/Bentley R & S-Series (Nutland)
Bluebird CN7 (Stevens)
BMC Competitions Department Secrets (Turner, Chambers & Browning)
BMW 5-Series (Cranswick)
BMW Z-Cars (Taylor)
BMW Boxer Twins 1970-1995 Bible, The (Falloon)
BMW – The Power of M (Vivian)
British Cars, The Complete Catalogue of, 1895-1975 (Culshaw & Horrobin)
BRM – A Mechanic's Tale (Salmon)
BRM V16 (Ludvigsen)
Bugatti Type 40 (Price)
Bugatti 46/50 Updated Edition (Price & Arbey)
Bugatti T44 & T49 (Price & Arbey)
Bugatti 57 2nd Edition (Price)
Bugatti Type 57 Grand Prix – A Celebration (Tomlinson)
Caravan, Improve & Modify Your (Porter)
Caravans, The Illustrated History 1919-1959 (Jenkinson)
Caravans, The Illustrated History From 1960 (Jenkinson)
Carrera Panamericana, La (Tipler)
Car-tastrophes – 80 automotive atrocities from the past 20 years (Honest John, Fowler)
Chrysler 300 – America's Most Powerful Car 2nd Edition (Ackerson)
Chrysler PT Cruiser (Ackerson)
Citroën DS (Bobbitt)
Classic British Car Electrical Systems (Astley)
Cobra – The Real Thing! (Legate)
Competition Car Aerodynamics 3rd Edition (McBeath)
Competition Car Composites A Practical Handbook (Revised 2nd Edition) (McBeath)
Concept Cars, How to illustrate and design (Dewey)
Cortina – Ford's Bestseller (Robson)
Cosworth – The Search for Power (6th edition) (Robson)
Coventry Climax Racing Engines (Hammill)
Daily Mirror 1970 World Cup Rally 40, The (Robson)
Daimler SP250 New Edition (Long)
Datsun Fairlady Roadster to 280ZX – The Z-Car Story (Long)
Dino – The V6 Ferrari (Long)
Dodge Challenger & Plymouth Barracuda (Grist)
Dodge Charger – Enduring Thunder (Ackerson)
Dodge Dynamite! (Grist)
Dorset from the Sea – The Jurassic Coast from Lyme Regis to Old Harry Rocks (also Souvenir Edition) (Belasco)
Draw & Paint Cars – How to (Gardiner)
Drive on the Wild Side, A – 20 Extreme Driving Adventures From Around the World (Weaver)
Dune Buggy, Building A – The Essential Manual (Shakespeare)
Dune Buggy Files (Hale)
Dune Buggy Handbook (Hale)
East German Motor Vehicles in Pictures (Suhr/Weinreich)
Fast Ladies – Female Racing Drivers 1888 to 1970 (Bouzanquet)
Fate of the Sleeping Beauties, The (op de Weegh/Hottendorff/op de Weegh)
Ferrari 288 GTO, The Book of the (Sackey)
Ferrari 333 SP (O'Neil)
Fiat & Abarth 124 Spider & Coupé (Tipler)
Fiat & Abarth 500 & 600 – 2nd Edition (Bobbitt)
Fiats, Great Small (Ward)
Ford Cleveland 335-Series V8 engine 1970 to 1982 – The Essential Source Book (Hammill)
Ford F100/F150 Pick-up 1948-1996 (Ackerson)
Ford F150 Pick-up 1997-2005 (Ackerson)
Ford GT – Then, and Now (Streather)
Ford GT40 (Legate)
Ford Midsize Muscle – Fairlane, Torino & Ranchero (Cranswick)
Ford Model Y (Roberts)
Ford Small Block V8 Racing Engines 1962-1970 – The Essential Source Book (Hammill)
Ford Thunderbird From 1954, The Book of the (Long)
Formula 5000 Motor Racing, Back then … and back now (Lawson)
Forza Minardi! (Vigar)
France: the essential guide for car enthusiasts – 200 things for the car enthusiast to see and do (Parish)
Grand Prix Ferrari – The Years of Enzo Ferrari's Power, 1948-1980 (Pritchard)
Grand Prix Ford – DFV-powered Formula 1 Cars (Robson)
GT – The World's Best GT Cars 1953-73 (Dawson)
Hillclimbing & Sprinting – The Essential Manual (Short & Wilkinson)
Honda NSX (Long)
Inside the Rolls-Royce & Bentley Styling Department – 1971 to 2001 (Hull)
Intermeccanica – The Story of the Prancing Bull (McCredie & Reisner)
Jaguar, The Rise of (Price)
Jaguar XJ 220 – The Inside Story (Moreton)
Jaguar XJ-S, The Book of the (Long)
Jeep CJ (Ackerson)
Jeep Wrangler (Ackerson)
The Jowett Jupiter – The car that leaped to fame (Nankivell)
Karmann-Ghia Coupé & Convertible (Bobbitt)
Kris Meeke – Intercontinental Rally Challenge Champion (McBride)
Lamborghini Miura Bible, The (Sackey)
Lamborghini Urraco, The Book of the (Landsem)
Lambretta Bible, The (Davies)
Lancia 037 (Collins)
Lancia Delta HF Integrale (Blaettel & Wagner)
Land Rover Series III Reborn (Porter)
Land Rover, The Half-ton Military (Cook)
Le Mans Panoramic (Ireland)
Lexus Story, The (Long)
Little book of microcars, the (Quellin)
Little book of smart, the – New Edition (Jackson)
Little book of trikes, the (Quellin)
Lola – The Illustrated History (1957-1977) (Starkey)
Lola – All the Sports Racing & Single-seater Racing Cars 1978-1997 (Starkey)
Lola T70 – The Racing History & Individual Chassis Record – 4th Edition (Starkey)
Lotus 18 Colin Chapman's U-turn (Whitelock)
Lotus 49 (Oliver)
Marketingmobiles, The Wonderful Wacky World of (Hale)
Maserati 250F In Focus (Pritchard)
Mazda MX-5/Miata 1.6 Enthusiast's Workshop Manual (Grainger & Shoemark)
Mazda MX-5/Miata 1.8 Enthusiast's Workshop Manual (Grainger & Shoemark)
Mazda MX-5 Miata, The book of the – The 'Mk1' NA-series 1988 to 1997 (Long)
Mazda MX-5 Miata Roadster (Long)
Mazda Rotary-engined Cars (Cranswick)
Maximum Mini (Booij)
Meet the English (Bowie)
Mercedes-Benz SL – R230 series 2001 to 2011 (Long)
Mercedes-Benz SL – W113-series 1963-1971 (Long)
Mercedes-Benz SL & SLC – 107-series 1971-1989 (Long)
Mercedes-Benz SLK – R170 series 1996-2004 (Long)
Mercedes-Benz SLK – R171 series 2004-2011 (Long)
Mercedes-Benz W123-series – All models 1976 to 1986 (Long)
Mercedes G-Wagen (Long)
MGA (Price Williams)
MGB & MGB GT– Expert Guide (Auto-doc Series) (Williams)
MGB Electrical Systems Updated & Revised Edition (Astley)
Micro Caravans (Jenkinson)
Micro Trucks (Mort)
Microcars at Large! (Quellin)
Mini Cooper – The Real Thing! (Tipler)
Mini Minor to Asia Minor (West)
Mitsubishi Lancer Evo, The Road Car & WRC Story (Long)
Montlhéry, The Story of the Paris Autodrome (Boddy)
Morgan Maverick (Lawrence)
Morgan 3 Wheeler – back to the future!, The (Dron)
Morris Minor, 60 Years on the Road (Newell)
Moto Guzzi Sport & Le Mans Bible, The (Falloon)
Motor Movies – The Posters! (Veysey)
Motor Racing – Reflections of a Lost Era (Carter)
Motor Racing – The Pursuit of Victory 1930-1962 (Carter)
Motor Racing – The Pursuit of Victory 1963-1972 (Wyatt/Sears)
Motor Racing Heroes – The Stories of 100 Greats (Newman)
Motorhomes, The Illustrated History (Jenkinson)
Motorsport In colour, 1950s (Wainwright)
MV Agusta Fours, The book of the classic (Falloon)
N.A.R.T. – A concise history of the North American Racing Team 1957 to 1983 (O'Neil)
Nissan 300ZX & 350Z – The Z-Car Story (Long)
Nissan GT-R Supercar: Born to race (Gorodji)
Northeast American Sports Car Races 1950-1959 (O'Neil)
Nothing Runs – Misadventures in the Classic, Collectable & Exotic Car Biz (Slutsky)
Pass the Theory and Practical Driving Tests (Gibson & Hoole)
Peking to Paris 2007 (Young)
Pontiac Firebird – New 3rd Edition (Cranswick)
Porsche Boxster (Long)
Porsche 356 (2nd Edition) (Long)
Porsche 908 (Födisch, Neßhöver, Roßbach, Schwarz & Roßbach)
Porsche 911 Carrera – The Last of the Evolution (Corlett)
Porsche 911R, RS & RSR, 4th Edition (Starkey)
Porsche 911, The Book of the (Long)
Porsche 911 – The Definitive History 2004-2012 (Long)
Porsche – The Racing 914s (Smith)
Porsche 911SC 'Super Carrera' – The Essential Companion (Streather)
Porsche 914 & 914-6: The Definitive History of the Road & Competition Cars (Long)
Porsche 924 (Long)
The Porsche 924 Carreras – evolution to excellence (Smith)
Porsche 928 (Long)
Porsche 944 (Long)
Porsche 964, 993 & 996 Data Plate Code Breaker (Streather)
Porsche 993 'King Of Porsche' – The Essential Companion (Streather)
Porsche 996 'Supreme Porsche' – The Essential Companion (Streather)
Porsche 997 2004-2012 – Porsche Excellence (Streather)
Porsche Racing Cars – 1953 to 1975 (Long)
Porsche Racing Cars – 1976 to 2005 (Long)
Porsche – The Rally Story (Meredith)
Porsche: Three Generations of Genius (Meredith)
Preston Tucker & Others (Linde)
RAC Rally Action! (Gardiner)
Racing Colours – Motor Racing Compositions 1908-2009 (Newman)
Racing Line – British motorcycle racing in the golden age of the big single (Guntrip)
Rallye Sport Fords: The Inside Story (Moreton)
Renewable Energy Home Handbook, The (Porter)
Roads with a View – England's greatest views and how to find them by road (Corfield)
Rolls-Royce Silver Shadow/Bentley T Series Corniche & Camargue – Revised & Enlarged Edition (Bobbitt)
Rolls-Royce Silver Spirit, Silver Spur & Bentley Mulsanne 2nd Edition (Bobbitt)
Rootes Cars of the 50s, 60s & 70s – Hillman, Humber, Singer, Sunbeam & Talbot (Rowe)
Rover P4 (Bobbitt)
Runways & Racers (O'Neil)
Russian Motor Vehicles – Soviet Limousines 1930-2003 (Kelly)
Russian Motor Vehicles – The Czarist Period 1784 to 1917 (Kelly)
RX-7 – Mazda's Rotary Engine Sportscar (Updated & Revised New Edition) (Long)
Singer Story: Cars, Commercial Vehicles, Bicycles & Motorcycle (Atkinson)
Sleeping Beauties USA – abandoned classic cars & trucks (Marek)
SM – Citroën's Maserati-engined Supercar (Long & Claverol)
Speedway – Auto racing's ghost tracks (Collins & Ireland)
Sprite Caravans, The Story of (Jenkinson)
Standard Motor Company, The Book of the (Robson)
Steve Hole's Kit Car Cornucopia – Cars, Companies, Stories, Facts & Figures: the UK's kit car scene since 1949 (Hole)
Subaru Impreza: The Road Car And WRC Story (Long)
Supercar, How to Build your own (Thompson)
Tales from the Toolbox (Oliver)
Tatra – The Legacy of Hans Ledwinka, Updated & Enlarged Collector's Edition of 1500 copies (Margolius & Henry)
Taxi! The Story of the 'London' Taxicab (Bobbitt)
To Boldly Go – twenty six vehicle designs that dared to be different (Hull)
Toleman Story, The (Hilton)
Toyota Celica & Supra, The Book of Toyota's Sports Coupés (Long)
Toyota MR2 Coupés & Spyders (Long)
Triumph TR6 (Kimberley)
Two Summers – The Mercedes-Benz W196R Racing Car (Ackerson)
TWR Story, The – Group A (Hughes & Scott)
Unraced (Collins)
Volkswagen Bus Book, The (Bobbitt)
Volkswagen Bus or Van to Camper, How to Convert (Porter)
Volkswagens of the World (Glen)
VW Beetle Cabriolet – The full story of the convertible Beetle (Bobbitt)
VW Beetle – The Car of the 20th Century (Copping)
VW Bus – 40 Years of Splitties, Bays & Wedges (Copping)
VW Bus Book, The (Bobbitt)
VW Golf: Five Generations of Fun (Copping & Cservenka)
VW – The Air-cooled Era (Copping)
VW T5 Camper Conversion Manual (Porter)
VW Campers (Copping)
Volkswagen Type 3, The book of the – Concept, Design, International Production Models & Development (Glen)
You & Your Jaguar XK8/XKR – Buying, Enjoying, Maintaining, Modifying – New Edition (Thorley)
Which Oil? – Choosing the right oils & greases for your antique, vintage, veteran, classic or collector car (Michell)
Works Minis, The Last (Purves & Brenchley)
Works Rally Mechanic (Moylan)

www.veloce.co.uk

First published in 2005 by Veloce Publishing Limited, Veloce House, Parkway Farm Business Park, Middle Farm Way, Poundbury, Dorchester DT1 3AR, England. Fax 01305 250479 / e-mail info@veloce.co.uk / web www.veloce.co.uk or www.velocebooks.com.
Reprinted March 2017. ISBN: 978-1-787110-92-2; UPC: 6-36847-01092-8.

British Library Cataloguing in Publication Data – A catalogue record for this book is available from the British Library. Typesetting, design and page make-up all by Veloce Publishing Ltd on Apple Mac. Printed and bound by CPI Group (UK) Ltd, Croydon, CR0 4YY.

HOW TO MODIFY
SUZUKI 4x4
FOR SERIOUS OFF-ROAD ACTION

John Richardson

VELOCE PUBLISHING
THE PUBLISHER OF FINE AUTOMOTIVE BOOKS

Veloce *SpeedPro* books –

978-1-903706-59-6

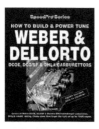

978-1-903706-75-6

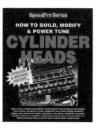

978-1-903706-76-3

978-1-903706-99-2

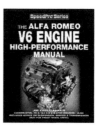

978-1-845840-21-1

978-1-845840-73-0

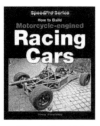

978-1-845841-23-2

978-1-845841-86-7

978-1-845841-87-4

978-1-845842-07-9

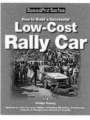

978-1-845842-08-6

978-1-845842-62-8

978-1-845842-89-5

978-1-845842-97-0

978-1-845843-15-1

978-1-845843-55-7

978-1-845844-33-2

978-1-845844-38-7

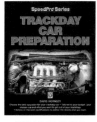

978-1-845844-83-7

978-1-845846-15-2

978-1-845848-33-0

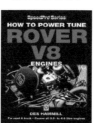

978-1-845848-68-2

978-1-845848-69-9

978-1-845849-60-3

978-1-845840-19-8

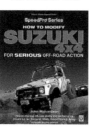

978-1-787110-92-2

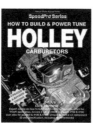

978-1-787110-47-2

978-1-903706-94-7

978-1-787110-87-8

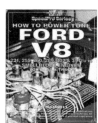

978-1-787110-90-8

978-1-787110-01-4

978-1-901295-26-9

978-1-845841-62-1

978-1-787110-91-5

978-1-787110-88-5

978-1-903706-78-7

Contents

Using this book & essential information

USING THIS BOOK

Throughout this book the text assumes that you, or your contractor, will have a workshop manual specific to your vehicle to follow for complete detail on dismantling, reassembly, adjustment procedure, clearances, torque figures, etc. This book's default is the standard manufacturer's specification for your vehicle type so, if a procedure is not described, a measurement not given, a torque figure ignored, you can assume that the standard manufacturer's procedure or specification for your engine should be used.

It is essential to read the whole book before you start work or give instructions to your contractor. This is because a modification or change in specification in one area can cause the need for changes in other areas. Get the whole picture so that you can finalise specification and component requirements as far as possible *before* any work begins.

ESSENTIAL INFORMATION

This book contains information on practical procedures; however, this information is intended only for those with the qualifications, experience, tools and facilities to carry out the work in safety and with appropriately high levels of skill. Whenever working on a car or component, remember that your personal safety must **ALWAYS** be your **FIRST** consideration. The publisher, author, editors and retailer of this book cannot accept any responsibility for personal injury or mechanical damage which results from using this book, even if caused by errors or omissions therein. If this disclaimer is unacceptable to you, please return the pristine book to your retailer who will refund the purchase price.

In the text of this book "**Warning!**" means that a procedure could cause personal injury and "**Caution!**" that there is danger of mechanical damage if appropriate care is not taken. However, be aware that we cannot foresee every possibility of danger in every circumstance.

Please note that changing component specification by modification is likely to void warranties and also to absolve manufacturers from any responsibility in the event of component failure and the consequences of such failure.

Increasing the engine's power will place additional stress on engine components and on the car's complete driveline: this may reduce service life and increase the frequency of breakdown. An increase in engine power, and therefore the vehicle's performance, will mean that your vehicle's braking and suspension systems will need to be kept in perfect condition and uprated as appropriate. It is also usually necessary to inform the vehicle's insurers of any changes to the vehicle's specification.

The importance of cleaning a component thoroughly before working on it cannot be overstressed. Always keep your working area and tools as clean as possible. Whatever specialist cleaning fluid or other chemicals you use, be sure to follow - completely - manufacturer's instructions, and if you are using petrol (gasoline) or paraffin (kerosene) to clean parts, take every precaution necessary to protect your body and to avoid all risk of fire.

Introduction & Acknowledgements

INTRODUCTION

It is no exaggeration to say that my life changed when I set foot in my first Suzuki 4x4. The go-anywhere ability, combined with its small size and low weight, was a revelation after my previous off-road vehicles. Muddy inclines that had once been impossible were conquered with ease. Of course, there were still places that the little machine could not go in standard form, which lead me to looking at modifying it to cope better, and the rest, as they say, is history.

My passion for modifying and driving the various Suzuki 4x4 models has brought many new friends and acquaintances, throughout the world; has lead me to found a Suzuki off-road club; and brought me the good fortune of being able write for one of the country's leading 4x4 magazines, *4X4 Mart*, which, ultimately, has resulted in the writing of this book.

The little 4x4's popularity is truly international, and it has large followings in the UK, USA, Australia, Europe and, of course, Asia. With new clubs and modifying companies springing up all the time, the future for off-roading the little Suzukis seems brighter than ever. The number of cheap, good condition, second-hand vehicles is also increasing every day, and the amount of modifying kit on the market is staggering compared to just a few years ago. The design of the vehicles themselves also lends itself to easy home modification, especially the leaf spring models, but today the amount of modification you undertake is only really limited by your free time and the depth of your pockets.

The number of Suzuki 4x4 fans across the world is ever increasing, as older models become more available, and growing numbers of first time off-roaders and old hands alike realise just how good these machines are in the rough. There has been much talk of 'hairdresser's cars' and the like over the years, but as more of the little off-roaders excel at Challenge and Trials events, the more mainstream they will become.

For future years the Jimny looks to be an exciting prospect, albeit not as simple to modify as the old SJ series. But with a few years head start, by the time the latest model is of an age to be available to the average off-road fanatic, there should be a plethora of kit on the market. Therefore, it looks hopeful that the Suzuki off-road following will continue to grow for many years to come.

The aim of this book is to enable a total novice to choose a suitable vehicle and plan the modifications required to build their ultimate off-roader in stages, yet still be able to enjoy their vehicle after each phase of development. I hope it will also be a useful reference for the more experienced modifier and that the examples on the following pages will inspire you to go on to even better things. You may not have the facilities, or even the inclination, to emulate the more extreme vehicles, but they can be a great source of ideas.

There is no other book that combines all the aspects of Suzuki off-road modifications in such depth, and if you are new to the Suzuki range, an old hand, or new to off-roading altogether, I hope these pages will help you see what is possible and inspire you to get involved. So, whether you just like tinkering with machines, or fancy the thrill of driving through seemingly impassable terrain, or both, there is no longer any excuse to sit around admiring other peoples' machines, so get out there and get on with your own.

ACKNOWLEDGEMENTS

I would like to take this opportunity to thank all of those in the Suzuki off-road community internationally that have contributed to this book. Although too numerous to mention by name your contribution of photographs and information has been invaluable.

In particular, I should like to thank my wife Jan, without whose love and support, this book, nor any of my other achievements in the world of off-roading would not have been possible; Damon Fisher for his continuous help and enthusiasm; and last, but not least, David Morton whose encouraging words sparked the whole thing off.

I hope you all enjoy the end result.

John Richardson

Chapter 1
Evolution

The first Suzuki 4x4 was launched in April 1970. The LJ10 (LJ standing for Light Jeep) or Jimny 360 as it was officially named, was a derivative of the Hope Star ON360, a tiny, no frills (such as doors) 4x4 built by the Hope Star Company in 1967. Production of the ON360 was limited, there being no more than 50 built, 30 of which were exported. In 1968 Suzuki gained the production rights and set about developing the design for the home market.

Due to Japanese vehicle regulations at the time the vehicle had to be small, which is why the spare wheel is mounted inboard so as not to make the vehicle too long, and the two-cylinder, two-stroke, air-cooled 359cc engine from the ON360 was retained, albeit now manufactured by Suzuki instead of Mitsubishi. Suzuki managed to increase the power output from 21bhp to 24bhp and added a few

Even after 35 years some LJ10s are still going strong. (Courtesy Chris Johnson)

refinements, such as its cylinder and crankshaft injection (CCI) lubrication system, which gave far superior lubrication and meant owners no longer had to mix their own two-stroke fuel.

The LJ50, with its 35bhp engine, was a definite step up. (Courtesy Brad Crisp)

The LJ50 and LJ55 had a 539cc three-cylinder, two-stroke engine. (Courtesy Brad Crisp)

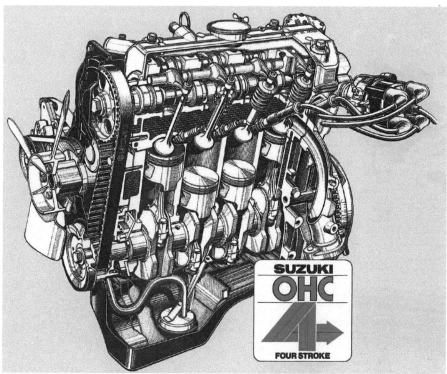

The 797cc four-cylinder, four-stroke was the first real engine of the range. (Courtesy Suzuki GB)

Two years later the L20 was launched. It had a water-cooled engine, producing a staggering 28bhp, and was the first of the line to have 15in wheels. Then came the LJ50 and LJ55 with a 539cc, three-cylinder, two-stroke engine giving 35bhp. The body also increased in size as the Japanese Mini Car regulations were relaxed, which also meant the spare could be externally-mounted.

Although the Japanese market was accustomed to such miniscule motors, it was obvious that if the vehicle was to stand any chance of being exported a larger engine would be necessary. During the next few years the motor evolved from the 550cc, two-stroke triple,

The LJ80 was a hit, and paved the way for the later Suzuki off-road models. (Courtesy Suzuki GB)

into the 41bhp, 797cc, four-cylinder four-stroke that eventually powered the LJ80. Launched in 1977 the LJ80 was the first of the diminutive 4x4s to be imported into the UK, although roughly three and a half thousand of the previous LJs had been sold in the US, and they were also extremely popular in Australia.

In 1978 Heron Suzuki GB set up Suzuki GB (Cars) Ltd, and imported a few test vehicles into the UK for potential customers with rural businesses. The farmers, etc. chosen to undertake the evaluation quickly realised the potential of the go-anywhere lightweight vehicle which easily handled terrain that defeated its heavyweight competition, a trait that today's Suzuki off-road fraternity put to best advantage.

With the success of the vehicle in Australia, where the young had adopted the little off-roader as a lifestyle vehicle, the whole emphasis of the export advertising changed, and the 'Wild Weekender' campaign began, suggesting that young, town-based couples could escape the urban jungle at weekends with wind in the hair motoring in the countryside. This image, combined with the emphasis of being able to cope in winter conditions that would have ordinary vehicles stranded, has been the baseline for the range ever since.

Whilst the LJ and its predecessors could hardly claim to have set the 4x4 world alight, it did instil in people's minds the principle of a small, utilitarian, go-anywhere vehicle from a Japanese manufacturer and opened the way for the success of future models, and in that respect its importance to the development of

The SJ410 surpassed all sales expectations, appealing to many different users.
(Courtesy Suzuki GB)

the Suzuki brand as a serious player on the 4x4 market should not be underestimated.

No-one, not even Suzuki itself, could have foreseen the explosion in popularity that would ensue with the launch of the SJ series. Launched just before the demise of the hot hatch fashion in the UK, following the insurance industry backlash against young drivers in fast cars, the 970cc SJ410 was quickly adopted as a yuppie icon and sales soared. This was not just a British phenomenon, however, and following deals with General Motors and Land Rover Santana SA, assembly lines were soon producing SJs in Canada and Spain, neatly avoiding the stringent import agreements of the time.

In 1986 the Samurai was launched in the US into a huge market just waiting for a small, rugged and cheap, four-wheel

drive vehicle. The initial reaction of the motoring press was greatly encouraging and its popularity grew rapidly, until 1988 when the Consumers Union launched a campaign against the little vehicle; a campaign which was only just resolved in 2004. Basically, the Consumers Union suggested that its tests had shown the little 4x4 had an alarming tendency to roll over. In the UK, following several nasty accidents where ex-hot hatch drivers had attempted to drive SJs in a similar manner to their previous vehicles, the Consumer's Association quickly jumped on the bandwagon, claiming that the vehicle should be banned.

It has since been proven in court, following action to obtain footage taken at the time, that these tests were, to be polite, seriously flawed. In the UK the Department of Transport undertook its own

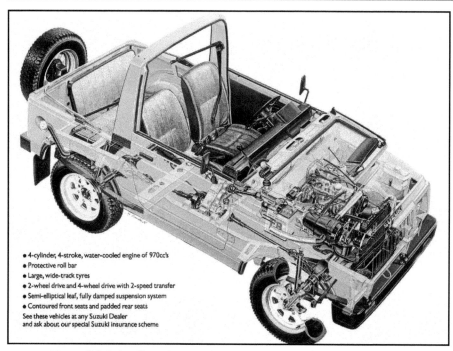

- 4-cylinder, 4-stroke, water-cooled engine of 970cc's
- Protective roll bar
- Large, wide-track tyres
- 2-wheel drive and 4-wheel drive with 2-speed transfer
- Semi-elliptical leaf, fully damped suspension system
- Contoured front seats and padded rear seats

See these vehicles at any Suzuki Dealer
and ask about our special Suzuki insurance scheme

**The stylish little off-roaders continued to sell, despite the negative press.
(Courtesy Suzuki GB)**

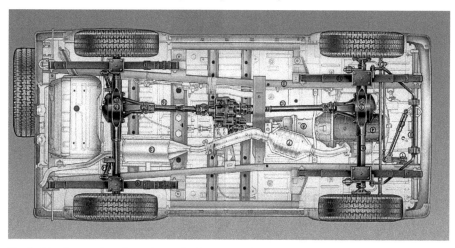

**The ladder frame chassis and transfer box transmission are a well proven combination.
(Courtesy Suzuki GB)**

even today the general public still view them with scepticism.

It's amazing, however, that during all this, although sales were seriously hit, the vehicle was still selling, and today's off-roaders can be grateful it was.

The SJ410 was the first of the new body shape, and formed the basis for the SJ413 and Samurai. The basic ladder chassis design was not unlike a small version of several other old style 4x4s, but where the Suzuki scored was on its size. Although having a similar wheelbase to, say, a SWB Land Rover, its smaller and lighter engine and components gave it the edge over its competitors by being economical, easy to handle in traffic, and so light it would 'float' over conditions that had more illustrious models struggling.

1987 saw the introduction of the Santana. Although not hugely different from the SJ410, the numerous little changes to power, handling, ride, gearbox and, probably most importantly, accessories, meant that Suzuki had a hit on its hands from the start.

The SJ410 was soon followed by the SJ413. Virtually indistinguishable from its smaller counterpart, except for the new grille and the bulge in the bonnet to accommodate the longer stroked engine, it was basically an upgraded SJ410 with a 1324cc detuned Swift engine. The 40% increase in power, however, meant that the new machine could just about cruise at the legal limit on a motorway, and its off-road performance was greatly improved, making it particularly popular with early modifiers.

In 1988 Suzuki introduced the far more civilised, coil sprung,

tests to resolve the issue and, sure enough, managed to roll over one of the test vehicles. It was not a Suzuki, however, and a statement was issued that basically said they were no more unstable than any other off-road vehicle, but advised all manufacturers of multi-purpose

vehicles to issue advisory notes to draw drivers' attention to their different handling characteristics. Unfortunately, though, the damage had been done and the press, not wishing to sully its pages with good news, hardly mentioned the exoneration of the little Suzuki, and

Despite its success with lifestyle vehicles Suzuki never forgot its commercial roots. (Courtesy Suzuki GB)

territory in the 4x4 market. This was no tarted-up commercial vehicle, this was a road going car first and foremost, but underneath its pretty exterior lurked the separate chassis and low range transfer box of a real off-roader. There is much to support the claim that this was the first of the 'lifestyle' off-road vehicles.

The early, 75bhp, 8-valve carburettored models soon received a small hike in power thanks to throttle body fuel injection, but the real shot in the arm came in the guise of the 16-valve engine, which boosted the power to 95bhp. No hot hatch, but ample performance for the type of vehicle, albeit still a little lacking in torque for a true off-roader.

There have been several revamps of the range, including the 4u, a very basic model with an engine and two seats and not much else, but it came with a long list of additional parts (such as the rear seats) that you could mix and match to build your own personalised vehicle.

The SJ413 was a big improvement on the SJ410, if only for the extra power.

The relative sophistication of the Vitara, with its responsive 1.6-litre engine and coil sprung suspension took Suzuki into completely new 1600cc-engined Vitara. With much of the appeal of its predecessor and few of the drawbacks, it had an altogether more 'small car' feel. Indeed, in 1989 *What Car Magazine* named it Best All-Terrain Car of the Year, and the unfortunate reputation of the SJ was finally laid to rest.

The Samurai was given wider track and bigger tyres, making it the ultimate leaf sprung Suzuki. (Courtesy Suzuki GB)

The Vitara was a whole new concept, with a 1.6-litre engine and coil sprung suspension.

During the mid-nineties the X-90 appeared, to all intents and purposes a two-seater Vitara with a boot, and this was available in two- and four-wheel drive.

In 1998 came the Grand Vitara, a much larger and more stylish vehicle than its predecessors. Over the last few years this has developed into the latest seven-seat, 2.7-litre V6, XL-7, which is a serious contender in the large SUV market.

The X-90 was a much berated but very capable model that, sadly, never really took off.

The original 75bhp, 8-valve Vitara power plant.

The Suzuki line-up would not be complete without the model I have deliberately left for last; the Jimny; a car which will in time become the Samurai of the 21st century. It is, in essence, the ultimate SJ, with a 1298cc engine delivering 79bhp and coil sprung suspension it comes somewhere between the SJ and the Vitara in design and ability.

Whilst it has serious competition from the likes of the Daihatsu Terios, the Jimny's superior styling and off-road prowess should see it through, and many have already been modified into superb off-roaders. So for anyone out there still mourning the demise of the Samurai, take heart, the Jimny will become a worthy replacement in time, and a common sight off-road, and will provide many a future modifier with a superb base machine on which to vent their imagination. We can only wait to see what Suzuki offers in the future, but if it stays with its past philosophy, it won't go far wrong.

Throttle body injection gave the 8-valve engine a power boost prior to the development of the 16-valve unit.

The Jimny could be regarded as the ultimate SJ.

The Vitara range took a step up with the launch of the Grand Vitara. (Courtesy Suzuki GB)

There are even some serious competition Jimnys about.
(Courtesy KAP Suzuki)

Several people are already modifying Jimnys, and the model's future looks bright. (Courtesy KAP Suzuki)

Chapter 2
The basics

PRINCIPLES OF MODIFICATION

All vehicle design is a compromise, and any modifications undertaken merely bias the compromise towards a particular aspect. For example, if you wish to race a saloon car you would have to significantly lower and increase the stiffness of the suspension to allow the vehicle to cope with cornering at high speed. However, this would have the effect of introducing harshness into the ride. Therefore, you have shifted the ratio from comfort towards handling for speed.

Off-road modification is no exception. Whether you wish to just potter about on easy green lanes with the family at weekends, immerse yourself in gallons of mud, or roar up Pike's Peak at breakneck speed, will determine the type and severity of the modifications you need to undertake.

All vehicle modification involves compromise relative to use.

Suzuki 4x4s were designed originally to provide a cheap, go-anywhere vehicle for Japan and the developing countries in Asia. The fact that they caught on in the West as an iconic lifestyle vehicle meant the designers had to rethink elements of the design to accommodate its new usage. These were mostly cosmetic initially, but eventually a wider stance, more power, softer suspension, and fashionable paintwork would all be included to boost sales in the West.

This book is primarily designed to allow you to determine what level of modification you need to achieve the performance you want. It will then help to decide whether to undertake these modifications yourself, by manufacturing and fitting your own parts, or source a supplier for the parts or to do the whole build for you, depending on your level of ability. For ease of reference there follows a description of the general principles of modification together with sections covering the usual usages to help you decide which is right for you.

General principles
Unless you are engaged in some form of off-road racing, it's safe to say there are only eight ways that

Approach and departure angles will both increase when the suspension or bodywork are raised.

The ramp breakover angle will decrease as the vehicle gets taller.

For off-road vehicles modifications should also be tailored to what you require from your vehicle.

your 4x4 will be brought to a stop:

1. Loss of traction due to slipping tyres
2. Loss of traction due to bottoming out
3. Cross-axling
4. Insufficient ramp breakover angle
5. Insufficient approach or departure angle
6. Mechanical failure or accident (i.e. breaking or hitting something)
7. Rolling over
8. Being submerged

Although it is highly likely you'll encounter one of the first five, changing the tyres will alleviate all five of these factors. Simply fitting larger radius tyres will raise the axles, chassis and bodywork and thus the ground clearance. This will assist with items 2-5 and, if you take the opportunity to fit more aggressive tread patterns as well, then the chances of item 1 occurring will also be decreased. The trade-off is that the propensity for item 7 to occur may be slightly increased. If, as is likely, the tyres are also wider, then the chances of rolling over will be significantly reduced, and fitting wheel spacers will reduce this even further.

It is possible to fit slightly larger, more aggressively-patterned tyres on standard rims and leave it at that, but although the gains are considerable, for a lot of people this is merely the start of a journey of modification that ends only when the money runs out. Also, the original bodywork will limit your choice of tyres.

This brings us to our next area

Hopefully you won't end up upside down, at least not to begin with.

is where the main axle housing, containing the differential, is attached to the shell of the vehicle, and the wheels are held in place by some framework, commonly called control arms, that allow them to move independently of the axle, whilst power is transmitted to the wheels by drive shafts fitted with constant velocity joints.

It's safe to say that, generally, coil sprung suspension is superior to leaf sprung. This is true for both handling and comfort. It can be argued, however, that there is one area where this is not necessarily the case, extreme off-roading. Whilst I would not suggest that leaf springs are superior to coils I would argue that they can be as effective, and they are easier and less expensive to maintain and modify.

Larger tyres will certainly be on your shopping list.

for modification; the suspension. There are two basic types of suspension on Suzuki four-wheel drives; leaf sprung suspension and coil sprung suspension. This can be further broken down into leaf sprung live axle, coil sprung live axle and coil sprung independent.

A live axle is hung from the suspension and moves up and

The front axle casing is bolted to the chassis with the independent suspension of the Vitara.

down as the suspension rides over obstacles. An independent set-up

It is also possible that, under certain conditions, an independently

With independent suspension the wheel is free to move independently of the main axle and the opposite wheel.

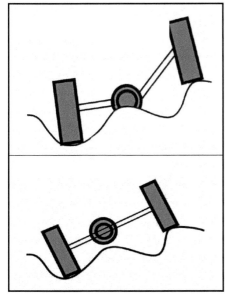

Independent suspension is not necessarily superior in all conditions. Top: independent suspension can cause the diff to lower. Bottom: With a beam axle, raising either wheel lifts the entire axle.

sprung wheel can rise over an obstacle without raising the axle and

differential, which, in turn, may then collide with an obstruction under the vehicle. With a live axle, on the other hand, everything lifts with the wheel and thus rises over the obstruction. This may be a small point but in extreme off-road, especially in rocky areas, it can be significant.

WHAT TO LOOK FOR IN A VEHICLE

The Suzuki range contains, without

The SJ410 is a great little vehicle but not the best choice as a base for radical modification.

doubt, some of the most competent vehicles you will encounter off-road. With their short wheelbase, ladder chassis, transfer box transmission, and light weight they are giant killers in the rough. There are now thousands of second-hand models around going for a song, which is good news for those of us who want to get muddy at the weekend, but, because of their very nature, a lot of these older vehicles have been abused and it is not unknown for them to suffer from corrosion. So, what do you look for if you're buying a second-hand Suzuki?

Well, let's start with the engine. If you think you'll want to modify your vehicle at some point, then it's best to avoid the 997cc engined varieties. SJ410s don't have sufficient power to drive much larger tyres, and they are significantly more difficult and more expensive to modify, as their engines and transmissions aren't compatible with

The 1.3-litre engine is not only more powerful than the 1.0-litre unit but has a number of other advantages when it comes to modification.

the larger-engined varieties. It's a common error amongst newcomers to the sport to think that a 1.3- or even a 1.6-litre engine will bolt straight in, they won't. So save yourself a lot of grief and go for the bigger-engined varieties from the start. Whilst these small engines may be fine for the type of driving for which they were originally designed, they are not particularly well suited for driving at 70mph on a motorway. Subsequently, the engines can get thrashed, and if they're not regularly serviced they will give up the ghost quite readily. Having said that, they are incredibly strong and reliable for their size, and if given a little tender loving care can take a huge amount of abuse.

Make sure you know which areas you intend to modify before viewing a potential purchase.

The good news is that the engines are so basic that even a novice should be able to spot a bad one. For example, a rattle, other than tappet noise on the top end, is likely to be a bearing on its last legs. A cloud of smoke from the exhaust, for example, especially on start up, is probably due to worn piston rings or valve guides. Either way avoid them, there are plenty more around. Be wary if the engine has been warmed up prior to your arrival. There may be a perfectly innocent reason for this, but starting problems due to a poor automatic choke, or even little end bearing rattle, can be concealed by a warm engine. Of course, if you intend to change the engine anyway, a rattling or smoking engine can bring you a bargain vehicle.

Suzuki engines can be prone to overheating. This is usually due to the radiator matrix being blocked with mud if the vehicle has been seriously off-roaded, although it's not unheard of for the radiator core to be blocked internally. Either way, it may

need to be replaced. **Caution!** – never pressure wash a mud blocked radiator, as the heat dissipating fins will be bent by the force of water and block the radiator more effectively and permanently than the mud you are attempting to remove. Instead, remove and soak the radiator in a caustic radiator cleaning solution for about a week, by which time gentle washing with a hose should remove most of the dirt.

Overheating could be a sign that the cylinder head gasket has blown, a not uncommon fault on any model. Look for emulsified oil in the oil filler cap, pressurisation of the cooling system, or a rough-running engine. Installing a new cylinder head gasket is not a huge job, but you must ensure you have the new gasket the right way up. It's possible to fit the gasket upside down, which will result in a severely restricted oil flow to the camshaft.

Alternators and starters can also be a problem if they've been subjected to deep water, but as a

rule they are generally reliable. Oil leaks are something to look out for; oil dripping from the base of the bellhousing, for example, could indicate a faulty crankshaft seal, which is a bit of a job to repair, though it's more likely to be either the rear of the rocker cover housing, where the gasket has blown, or the distributor gasket, check for this by tracking the oil back to its source. Neither are huge jobs, but should all be reflected in the price.

Another area to check is the weep hole at the base of the petrol pump. If there is a trail of oil issuing from here it means the fuel pump seal has gone and you ignore it at your peril. A leak that may appear small when stationary will pump out unbelievable amounts of oil when you are moving at speed, and will quickly leave you with a dry sump and a seized engine.

Automatic chokes are prone to problems when they get a bit long in the tooth, and many fruitless hours can be spent trying to rectify

The mechanical fuel pump is one item you ignore at your peril.

mysterious starting and running problems. It's better by far to fit a manual choke conversion, or even replace the entire unit with a Weber or Nikki carb conversion.

The transmission is normally fairly bulletproof. Differential bearings can be a problem, though,

particularly the rear, for obvious reasons, especially if the vehicle has been taken into deep water with the original poppet type axle breathers which can allow water ingress into the axle housing. Prop shaft universal joints can also be prone to failure.

To check the diff bearings, try to move the prop shaft up and down and side to side near the front of the diff. Any movement will mean the bearing is on the way out. If possible, check the axle oil, if it's a nice yellow sludge, you have a problem and the oil needs to be replaced immediately. To check the universal joint, twist the prop shaft in either direction and check for movement between the yokes on either side of the universal joint. Some movement in the diff itself when rotating the shaft is quite normal.

Original dampers will definitely need to be replaced.

Whilst you are underneath the vehicle, check the dampers for leaks and operation. Dampers on an off-roader take some serious punishment, and it's likely that ordinary road units will need replacing within a year or two if the vehicle has been in the rough. Dampers will probably last for 30,000 miles or so of normal use, but unless they look fairly new I would replace them almost as a matter of course. They are not that expensive and, to be fair, the ride can do with all the help it can get. Of course, if you're intending to modify the vehicle it would be best to wait until a decision has been made regarding damper size and performance before replacement.

The springs on a 15 year old vehicle will almost certainly be worn out, with that distinctive concave look. This will not help the handling

Replacing the automatic choke with a manual conversion can save a lot of grief.

Replacing tired leaf springs can give your vehicle a new lease of life.

either on or off-road. New springs can be had reasonably cheaply, but beware, some modified lift springs are like rock and give no benefit whatever, other than lifting the vehicle body. Although this can be advantageous for off-roading, lifting springs are only truly an advantage if they flex freely as well.

If you are used to a comfortable modern saloon car the ride and handling of a leaf sprung Suzuki may come as something of a shock. It can be reasonably described as back jarring, especially the older SJ410. There was also a lot of scaremongering in the press a few years ago about the Samurai's propensity to roll over. Whilst this is not without a grain of truth, the vehicle is certainly no worse than the majority of 4x4s. It ought to go without saying that a vehicle with a raised centre of gravity, such as found in the Suzuki 4x4 range,

requires a different driving style than a sports car, and should, therefore, be driven accordingly.

The area that lets down more Suzukis than any other is, without doubt, the bodywork. Below is a

Finding an older vehicle without rust is fairly unlikely.

list of areas that are susceptible to rust. It would probably be quicker to say the only place that doesn't rust is the roof, although you can only guarantee that on a soft-top!

The particular areas to watch out for are:

● There is a good chance that the sills, both inner and outer, are starting to corrode; those plastic trims can hide a multitude of sins. Check under the carpet, and underneath the vehicle along the entire length of each sill. The ends of the sills, beneath the wheelarches, especially at the rear, also require a thorough check.

The sills are a prime area to look for corrosion.

● The wheelarches, where the inner and outer wings meet around the wheels and the lower front corner of the wing over the end of the bumper. Find an old one without any rust here and you have a rare beast indeed, or one that has had some serious work done to it. Lift the plastic trims and check underneath, and lift the bonnet and check inside the arches.
● The front inner wheelarches, especially at their connection to the front floor.

All the wheelarches rot, especially along the seams.

The soft-top windscreen surround can be difficult to inspect without being dropped.

• The windscreen surround, which drops onto the bonnet on soft-top models, will almost certainly be rusty at the bottom and sides, and it's not cheap to replace. Ask for the screen to be dropped, and check the bottom of the panel where it seals to the top of the bulkhead. This area

isn't visible from outside the vehicle, and it's particularly susceptible to rust.

• Adjacent to the windscreen pillars the front bulkhead/door pillar corrodes just above, and in front of, the top door hinge.

• The bottoms of the doors; it's not unknown for the frame to be separated from the outer skin underneath.

Check the underside of all doors.

• On the off-side, the rear floor around the petrol filler pipe is prone to corrosion, but, because of the inner panel, this can normally only be checked from underneath. The rear floor where the fibre pads are fitted between the floor and the top of the chassis rails, and the rear seam beneath the back door that holds the door seal, are yet more areas to inspect.

• The rear wheelarches rot in a similar fashion to those at the front. Adjacent to the front end of each arch is the rear slope of the cab floor. This is double-skinned, and is prone to rot at the seam at the top of the slope. This area needs to be

The rear floor around the fuel filler pipe is prone to corrosion and should be inspected from below.

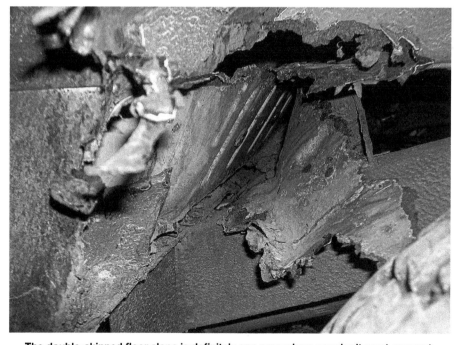

The double-skinned floor slope is definitely one area where you don't want any rust.

the captive body mount bolt, and the whole area is prone to rust, and particularly nasty to repair.

• The bottom seat belt mounts, particularly the one on the transmission tunnel, will be an MOT failure at best and a death-trap at worst if there is any corrosion. Whilst checking the seat belt mounts, have a good look at the handbrake mount on the transmission tunnel. This is an obvious stress point which can induce corrosion. I have known handbrake handles to tear out of the floor whilst being applied!

Seat belt mounting points should be rigorously inspected.

• The front and rear bumpers are a haven for mud and salty water from winter roads, and they corrode accordingly. The light units also get more than their fair share of abuse, and the connectors on the front sidelight and rear light units are prone to corrosion. If they corrode through you will need to buy a whole new unit, as they are practically impossible to repair.

• The rear fog lights, so buy a new one and fit it onto the rear door. It may be a bit higher, but that's better than having it ripped off or rattled

checked inside and out, as does the joint at the bottom of the slope,

behind the front seats. The bottom of the double-skinned area houses

Bumpers, light units, and especially rear fog lights, are probably best replaced with units more suitable to off-roading.

windows also become brittle and crack. Whilst soft-tops are not designed to last forever, they are expensive to replace and should be considered in the price of the vehicle. If purchasing an aging model as a base for modification, a new soft-top may well cost more than the vehicle.

If all this has made you think again then don't despair. The chassis on any Suzuki 4x4 is generally very good, and you'll be unlucky to find a rotten one, although strenuously off-roaded vehicles can show signs of fatigue. Of course, you'd be stupid not to check, but if the rest of the vehicle is okay, the chances are the chassis will be fine.

Don't get too hung up on mileage either, a well looked after example with 100,000 on the clock may well be a better buy than a

Soft-tops become worn out after a few years and are expensive to replace.

A new soft-top can rejuvenate a tired looking vehicle.

to pieces the first time you take it off-road.
• A soft-top that is more than 5 years old will almost certainly be showing signs of distress. Zips break, poppers tear out, and the material itself becomes brittle and rips around stress areas. The

thrashed, neglected model with less than half that mileage.

GREEN LANING
This is likely to be the least dramatic of off-road experiences and, as such, requires little or no modification to any Suzuki 4x4, other

Driving country lanes can be a very satisfying form of off-roading.

Minor vehicle preparation, such as waterproofing the ignition, is necessary for green laning.

Some green lanes are neither green nor lanes!

than, perhaps, more aggressively-patterned tyres. This is after all the kind of terrain they were designed to cope with. That said, there are green lanes in the UK that are neither green, nor lanes. So beware, what appears on a map as a pleasant country lane may have been turned into a sea of slimy rutted mud, churned up by farmers' tractors and machinery. It is fashionable at present to pillory green lane drivers for defacing the countryside, but experience shows that, with the exception of a few individuals, green lane drivers contribute to keeping lanes open to the public and free from obstructions, either natural or man made.

Note! – The debate on green laning in the UK continues so you should also be aware that it is now the obligation of the green lane driver to prove that they are legally entitled to be on the lane in question. It is not incumbent upon the landowner to prove that you should not. It is also possible for you to be prosecuted, fined, and have your vehicle confiscated, on the say so of any member of the public who should take your vehicle details and report you. Why this excessively draconian legislation should apply specifically to those of the green laning fraternity is unclear, but you have been warned. At present there

For recovery purposes, always go off-road with at least one other vehicle.

A body lift is an inexpensive way of getting bigger tyres under your vehicle.

stick to those three rules and you will be surprised what you can achieve, even in a standard vehicle.

The next area for attention is the tyres. It's generally possible to go up two sizes of tyre without any other modification. Combine this with a more aggressive tread pattern, such as an All-Terrain or a mild Mud-Terrain tyre, and you'll be pleasantly surprised at the increase in off-road performance, whilst not significantly reducing the on-road performance or handling. A reduction in performance can be especially noticeable on the smaller-engined vehicles, though these don't exactly have an excess of power to begin with.

To allow significantly larger tyres to be fitted, the initial modification I would suggest for either coil or leaf sprung vehicles is the body lift. This is the most cost-effective way of lifting the bodywork clear of any larger wheels and tyres, and allows you to go up another tyre size or two.

I'd set a limit of 3in (75mm) for a body lift. This will allow significantly larger tyres but will not require any further modification other than fitting the body spacers. Any more will start to seriously affect the handling of the vehicle, and won't give much more in the way of clearance, unless taken to ridiculous extremes.

MILD OFF-ROAD

To take the modifications one step further a mild form of suspension lift will be required. For leaf sprung vehicles this means longer shackles. It should be noted, though, that larger wheels will almost certainly be necessary as well at this stage.

Long shackles are the simplest and cheapest form of suspension

is also legislation in the pipeline to significantly reduce the amount of lanes that can be driven on, so you need to be sure of your facts.

The general rules to follow when green laning are: make certain your vehicle is in good condition; that

the ignition is waterproofed by an application of sealant spray; and that you have some form of recovery available, preferably in the form of one or more accompanying vehicles equipped with a towrope. These aren't modifications, of course, but

Long shackles are a common means of lifting the body on leaf sprung vehicles.

On coil sprung vehicles longer springs are a relatively inexpensive and simple suspension modification.

Ensure that coil lifting springs are longer, similarly rated springs rather than just heavy-duty springs.

modification. To raise the body one inch above the axle you'll need to lengthen the shackles by two inches. Because the leaf spring is hinged at one end, to increase the distance travelled halfway along its length (i.e. where the axle is positioned)

you need to increase the distance at the end of the spring by twice the amount. There are some good long shackles available commercially, but it is quite possible to make your own. For a simple one inch lift, two pieces of steel bar, two inches longer than the original shackle, with appropriate holes drilled in them will suffice. Any further height will require some form of welded cross-bracing, but I wouldn't condone going any more than a two inch lifting shackle (i.e. four inches longer than standard) even for entirely off-road applications.

If you have a coil sprung vehicle then you can purchase a set of lifting springs. A number of manufacturers supply lifting coil springs at the moment, but beware, as one particular set lifts purely by making stronger springs which do not compress as easily as normal and, although they do give you lift they also wreck the amount of articulation, which is just as important as the ground

clearance you are trying to create by fitting the springs in the first place. What you need is a set of longer springs with the same compression characteristics as the originals, but with more coils. Such springs can give you a two inch suspension lift very economically, although you'll also need to change to longer dampers to gain the full benefit.

For simple off-roading this is about the full extent of modification you will require, though you may wish to fit some vehicle recovery points and perhaps even a winch for self-recovery, depending on how bad the terrain is that you envisage traversing. For what would be classed as difficult green lanes, however, the above modifications should be ample. In fact, it would be possible to attempt a lot of off-road sites without being totally embarrassed with no more modification. But be warned, if you do, you'll almost certainly come away wanting more, much more.

SERIOUS OFF-ROAD AND TRIALS
This section is all about tackling very difficult terrain, yet still retaining a road legal capacity for the vehicle. The type of terrain will depend on where in the world you live. If you are in the US, for example, then you may be confronted with desert and rocks, mud and deep snow, and anything in between. In the UK, on the other hand, it's fair to say that you'll predominantly be faced with deep mud and water. One thing all extreme terrains have in common is the modifications required to enable your vehicle to cope. As discussed in the previous sections of this chapter the main principles are better ground clearance, better

In the UK you're most likely to encounter deep mud and water.

LONGER SHACKLES

Longer shackles, as covered in the Mild Off-Road section, should only be used up to a maximum of two inches of lift (i.e. four inch longer shackles). This should be an absolute limit, especially if the vehicle is going anywhere near a public highway, any longer than this is inherently dangerous. Not only do the vehicle's steering angles start to depreciate rapidly beyond this point but the stresses imparted into the springs, bushes, shackle bolts and chassis rails, as well as the shackles themselves, increase dramatically the longer the shackles become. This can manifest itself initially as

grip and better articulation. These principles, with some variations, are true for all disciplines, except, of course, the speed events, which will only be covered in passing.

The next step up the modification ladder for leaf sprung models is mainly dependent upon two things: terrain, and, more likely, budget. The six major principle designs are as follows.

LIFTING LEAF SPRINGS

Longer, more flexible springs are a good way of getting that necessary lift. Not only do they raise the vehicle but, by their very nature, they are more flexible, thus significantly increasing the potential articulation. They are easy to fit, needing little or no experience, and can be combined with many other modifications to give an additional suspension lift. It's probable that the springs on your SJ/Samurai will have seen better days in any case, appearing rather more concave than convex, new longer springs will instantly transform your vehicle and

Lifting leaf springs not only give better ground clearance, but also allow greater articulation.

can be added to at a later date with an additional modification when time or budget allow and I would suggest are worthy of consideration as the initial modification for any project.

dramatic steering wander, and ultimately as catastrophic failure. Attempting to drive at speed with the suspension no longer attached to the vehicle will ruin your day.

ELONGATING SHACKLES

These are not to be confused with longer shackles as covered in the previous section. There have been many designs of elongating, or missing link, shackles, the latest of which is simply a hinge, kept at the correct height whilst closed, with a nylon bump stop.

The basic principle is a two-piece shackle, hinged near the

Flexing shackles can give huge amounts of articulation. (Courtesy Rhino Central)

Hingeing shackles give a little lift when closed making bodywork modifications necessary if large tyres are to be fitted.

centre, that under normal conditions sites the spring at approximately the same height below the hanger as

the original shackle. Once the wheel encounters a significant hollow, however, the axle can drop as the hinge opens under the weight of the wheel and axle. The articulation possible with these shackles is very significant and only really limited by the stiffness of the spring. Combined with some new flexible springs, the articulation is enormous.

One drawback is that the shackles provide no lift under normal circumstances. It is, therefore, necessary to combine them with either a body lift or some severe modifications to the bodywork to enable much bigger than standard tyres to be fitted. They can also be combined with spring over axle lift. However, if the bodywork modification alone is undertaken, vehicle stability will be much better than on most modified vehicles as the ride height will have been increased by only the extra height of the tyres.

There are also similar designs available that combine the articulating shackle with a twisting mechanism which prevents the axle movement being limited by the spring's lateral stiffness.

SHACKLE REVERSAL

Some manufacturers now supply shackle reversal kits, which work on the principle that it is better to hinge the front leaf springs at the front of the spring as opposed to the rear, as on the standard truck. This has the effect of allowing the axle to lift as the wheels trail over obstacles. To achieve this, turrets are bolted through the original front spring hangers that form a framework to accept the front spring bush as the static mount, and specially-shaped shackles are installed to the rear of

The shackle reversal raises the suspension and gives a significantly superior ride.

the spring that mount into the rear spring hanger. As you are lifting both ends of the spring by approximately one and a half inches, the axle is thus lowered by one and a half inches (i.e. giving one and a half inches of lift). To realign the rear suspension, longer shackles are supplied.

Whilst not the most radical of off-road modifications this does significantly increase the articulation and gives a greatly superior ride, especially on the road, over the standard set-up; which, it must be said, is rather 'agricultural'. It also gives you one and a half inches of suspension lift over standard.

SPOA (SPRING PERCH OVER AXLE)

This apparently simple modification places the axles under the springs instead of over them, giving an immediate five inches of lift for seemingly little outlay. However, as with so much in this world, you don't get something for nothing.

The spring perches are welded to the underside of the axle tubes. To enable your springs to be re-located to the top of the tube some form of new perch will have to be fabricated. Traditionally either the old perches were carefully removed from the axle tube and re-welded to the top or replaced with newly fabricated perches. The trouble is, unless special care is taken to ensure the perches are correctly positioned, all sorts of problems are encountered with the steering geometry. Whilst this is not a huge problem at the

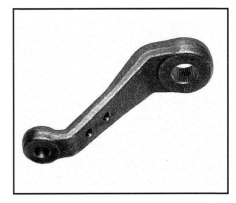

A drop Pitman arm or some other steering modification will be necessary with an SPOA conversion. (Courtesy Calmini)

low speeds encountered off-road, it is a big problem at moderately high speed on the road. Combined with the raised centre of gravity of the vehicle and knobbly tyres this modification can be lethal if undertaken incompetently.

The problems don't stop there either because the axle, and thus the steering rods, have been distanced from the chassis and the steering box, and the Pitman arm is, therefore, no longer man enough for the job. This can be overcome in two ways: either with a Z-bar, which elongates and raises the depth of the steering rod; or by using a drop Pitman arm, which is simply a replacement elongated Pitman arm that drops the link back down to its original position.

The drop Pitman arm is probably the best solution, but the Z-bar is far easier to manufacture in the home workshop, comprising, as it does, three sections of tube, a steel plate, and two adjustable track rod ends. If you're confident enough of your welding skills to build a major steering linkage then this will be by far the cheapest solution.

There are some kits available now that utilise the bottom perches

A spring over axle conversion is not as simple as it seems, but done correctly can transform your vehicle.

Ensure that a SPOA conversion is executed correctly as poor conversions can be a deathtrap.

as a form of stabiliser for a bracket that encompasses the axle tube, which is all held in place with U-bolts. On the face of it at least, this seems a reasonable and cost effective solution to the problem.

If you decide to proceed down this route you will, of course, also require significantly longer shocks. If you decide to re-use the original spring perches, then you'll also have to move the shock-mounts to enable the new shocks to be fitted.

There are many off-road vehicles that have this suspension set-up as standard, so it's not inherently dangerous if manufactured correctly, but a lot of home-made modifications are simply accidents waiting to happen.

COIL CONVERSION

Although it's possible to convert a leaf sprung vehicle to coil springs, this should not be attempted by the novice mechanic. If done

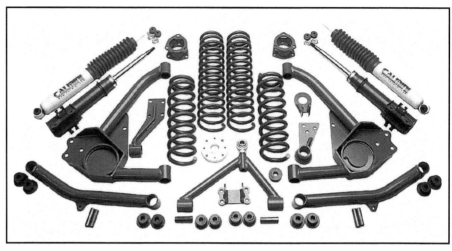

For serious off-roading Vitaras, Calmini's lifting suspension system is a must.
(Courtesy Calmini)

professionally, however, it gives great flexibility to the suspension setup and a far better ride. For speed events it is almost imperative that coil springs are employed. There were some coil sprung Samurais produced but, at least in the UK, you will be extremely fortunate to come across one of these.

COIL SUSPENSION LIFT KITS

Other than the lifting springs previously mentioned, it is difficult to modify the independent suspension setup simply. There are a few suspension kits on the market but these effectively trash the entire suspension system and replace it with newly-manufactured components. These can be obtained in two or three inch lift formats, although it's difficult to see why, if you are going to the trouble of replacing the whole suspension, you would opt for the two inch kit.

The major drawback with these kits is cost. As you can imagine, a kit containing an entirely new suspension system doesn't come cheap. Another potential outlay will be the plethora of new front differentials you will get through as, without additional modification, the three inch lifting kit can eat front differentials. Put a decent amount of torque through it in off-road conditions and the front diff mount rips out of the casing. Hardly surprising as it's only aluminium. There was one particular model of GV that had a steel-cased housing, but

A coil spring conversion can be a huge improvement.

finding one of these at a breakers is unlikely, to say the least. Fortunately there is a modification available now that limits the amount of stress imparted to the casing thus reducing the likelihood of damage occurring.

Replacement steel axles are also available, but this significantly increases the cost of an already expensive system, though the additional outlay will soon be recouped from the saving in replacement front differentials.

LIVE AXLES

If the suspension lift kit does not give sufficient potential then it's possible to fit a Samurai front axle to the front of an independently sprung vehicle. This can be either coil or leaf mounted and, combined with a simple bracket reversal on the rear springs, can give a huge amount of lift. This modification is only for those with a certain amount of expertise and a well-equipped workshop.

GEARING

If you opt for any suspension/tyre change that takes you over 29in tyres, then without some serious lowering of the gear ratios your original engine is going to struggle. The usual ways of overcoming this are to fit an SJ410 transfer box into a 1300cc engined model for up to 31in tyres and a combination of that and/or Vitara differentials for larger rubber. It is also possible to buy components to re-gear differentials and transfer boxes if you have sufficient funds.

ENGINE SWAPS

Another way round the lack of power is to fit a replacement engine. The 1600cc Vitara engine is a popular swap into the 1300cc engined variants. It is not a straight bolt-in swap, but not far off. There are various kits around that have an adaptor plate to fit.

Another popular engine swap is the Vauxhall/GM 2.0-litre twin cam, which gives a large increase in power and just about fits into the engine bay. Of course, as long as it comes from a rear-wheel drive car, it's just about possible to fit anything so long as it has its gearbox attached. There are

With a suitable conversion kit the 1.6-litre Vitara engine is a simple swap for the 1.3-litre unit. (Courtesy Calmini).

many examples of V6 and V8 engine conversions around, which are covered in chapter 9.

LIMITED SLIP DIFFS AND LOCKERS

With all that power on tap it's amazing the number of machines that still wave spinning wheels in the air. Fitting a diff locker of some description will help prevent wheel spin and loss of traction, and will keep you going where a truck with a standard diff will just flail about. There are various types around, the most popular probably being

A limited slip differential can be useful off-road but a diff locker is probably better. (Courtesy Calmini)

A less expensive, though technically more challenging modification is the live axle conversion.

the Detroit E-Z Locker, which has a spring loaded gear which can move when the diff is stressed, when cornering on-road, for example, but if traction is lost on one wheel on the axle with the locker installed all power is then transferred to the wheel with traction. A simple but effective means of overcoming the problem, although they can be very different to drive on-road, and the handling characteristics of the vehicle will change significantly.

A limited slip differential gives, on the face of it, a similar performance but uses a series of clutch plates and is a more refined piece of kit, which is reflected in the price, being roughly twice that of an E-Z Locker. This is not the full story, however, as an LSD does allow some movement, and thus loss of traction in extreme circumstances. For example, if you were to keep the vehicle in two-wheel drive, jack up one rear wheel on an axle with a LSD fitted, chock the front wheels and try driving away, the vehicle would not move. Try the same thing with a diff locker and, tyre traction permitting, the vehicle would simply drive over the obstacle. I trust it is obvious now why diff lockers are better suited to extreme off-roading.

Lockers are also available that use compressed air to insert a pin into the diff, which totally locks it when required. As you might guess these kits are quite expensive and require a certain amount of expertise to fit, so aren't very common on Suzukis.

A V8 coil sprung Samurai can be an attractive proposition. (Courtesy Steve Abbot)

RE-CHASSISING

If none of the above gives you what you're looking for, then it's possible to shorten the chassis from a larger vehicle, such as a Range Rover or Toyota, and replace the body with a Suzuki shell. I'm not sure how I feel about this, and it's obviously out of the question for purists, but I can see the appeal of a 3.5-litre V8 Samurai

This type of modification may sound out of reach but it's not as difficult as it might first appear, and can be achieved by a reasonably experienced mechanic on a budget akin to some of the other major modifications. The good news in the UK is that as you are reusing an existing chassis, single vehicle approval (SVA) is unnecessary, thus avoiding a costly and time-consuming procedure.

This about covers the mainstream types of modification and hopefully gives you an insight into what's possible and what's right for you. Obviously, it's possible to build whatever your imagination can come up with, but my intention was to stay within what is achievable for the home mechanic. I've avoided giving prices, as they are obviously fluid, and up to date figures can usually be found on suppliers' websites.

Chapter 3
Skills & equipment

This chapter is predominantly designed for total novices. How much you can achieve at home will, obviously, depend to a large extent on your skills base and workshop equipment, although you can achieve quite a lot with a standard tool kit on a driveway. The main thing is that you work safely. For instance, if you're raising the vehicle then a set of axle stands is an absolute must. A level working area, preferably concrete, is also required. During the rest of the chapter I shall highlight what I believe to be the best ways to undertake the various procedures. I won't insist on expensive purchases, but certain pieces of equipment are essential if you are to outlast your project.

EQUIPMENT
Axle stands
The larger the base area the more stable they are. Flat bases are

Axle stands should be strong with a large, firm base.

Crowbars have all sorts of uses and can be invaluable.

essential, the design which has steel angle placed end onto the floor will cut into anything but the hardest surface and become unstable as a result. It's the same with jacks; remember that the underside of your vehicle is much higher than normal and buy accordingly.

Crowbars
Various sizes of crowbar (prybar) are necessary for levering components in and out, and holding items in position during fitting.

These bars have a multitude of other uses also.

Basic tool kit
The best advice is to buy the best tools you can afford. Generally speaking, sets are better value if you're just starting out. A good set of tools, well looked after, will last you a lifetime, and beyond. I regularly use tools passed down to me by my father and grandfather.

Note! – Don't buy cheap spanners (wrenches) or sockets; not only will they not last, but you run the risk of doing yourself a serious injury if they fail under load. It is also very frustrating using tools that are not up to the job. The following list of tools will allow you to do most things on a Suzuki four-wheel drive:

• A set of metric combination spanners from 8-19mm. Ensure your set has a 15mm. These are quite often left out of sets and are used regularly on Suzukis. If money permits buy two sets, there are many instances when you will require two spanners of the same size and a socket will not fit.
• A set of half inch drive metric sockets, 8-19mm. There are instances when larger sockets will be necessary but these can be purchased individually later.
• A set of quarter inch drive, long-reach metric sockets, 6-13mm.
• A set of screwdrivers. A large, medium, small, stubby and electrical, in both cross head and flat blade are essential, preferably including a double ended offset crosshead and flat bladed screwdriver for areas with limited access.
• A set of Allen (hexagon) keys.
• 12 volt electrical circuit tester.
• Cable stripper and crimper.
• Normal engineers, and long nosed, pliers.
• Mole grips, Stillsons or a pipe wrench.
• Craft knife.
• Hacksaw and junior hacksaw.

Note! – A socket set is deemed to include a ratchet, T-bar, long and

short extension bars, and a universal joint as standard.

Chisels and drifts
Cold chisels are useful in various areas; loosening stubborn components and bolts, for example. Drift bars are used to knock bolts or other components out of sleeves and holes.

Circlip pliers
An inexpensive piece of kit, but essential for removing and fitting internal and external circlips.

Compression tester
Used to measure the pressure in the engine cylinders, and thus their condition. If the pressure is low, for example, then either the piston rings/bores are in need of attention, or the valves are not seating correctly.

If you want to get a good idea of an engine's internal condition you'll need a compression tester.

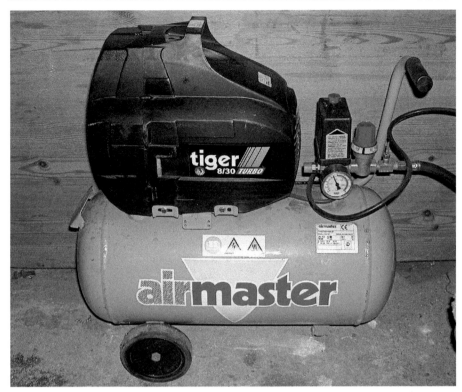

A compressor is not essential but prices have fallen dramatically and they are now within reach of most home mechanics.

Compressor and air tools

Compressors have come down in price and are now available to most hobby workshops. This will have many advantages over a purely electrical workshop. For instance, a compressor will enable you to pump up tyres, blow out blocked components, spray paint, and use a plethora of tools designed for compressed air, such as air chisels for cutting off panels. If you will be attempting any major modifications, then a compressor is worthy of serious consideration.

Dwell meter

A dwell meter is essential to set up mechanical ignition points correctly. It measures the angle of the rotation of the distributor shaft whilst the

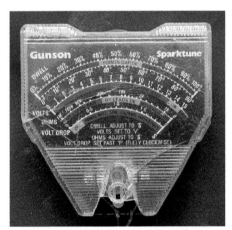

The dwell meter measures the angle of the rotation of the distributor shaft whilst the points are open, and allows accurate adjustment.

points are open, which determines the amount of electrical energy stored in the capacitor and thus sent to the spark plugs. If the points

are incorrectly set then your ignition system will run inefficiently. Dwell meters are easily obtainable and relatively inexpensive. Most later vehicles have contact-less ignition making a dwell meter unnecessary.

Hammers

Small, medium and large ball pein hammers are essential. A 2lb lump hammer can also be useful for removing stubborn transmission and suspension components.

Jacks

Best by far are trolley jacks. Bear in mind that, especially once you have modified your vehicle, any jacking point will be way off the ground. An ordinary home trolley jack for a small saloon car will probably not even reach the jacking point let alone raise the vehicle. There are specially produced 4x4 trolley jack models available now at a similar cost to an ordinary model. Check the manufacturer's maximum lift height against your vehicle.

Bottle jacks are okay. However, they are inherently not as stable as trolley jacks, and the higher you go the less stable they become. They should only be used for one wheel at a time, and an axle stand should be placed under the appropriate wheel as soon as possible.

A trolley jack with a high lift capacity will be required, especially after any suspension modifications.

The scissor jack supplied with the vehicle is for emergency use only, for changing a wheel, for example, and under no circumstances should it be used for workshop activities.

Panel beating set

A twin-headed, flat and rounded panel hammer, and universal and flat dolly blocks should be sufficient for most jobs. Body jacking equipment is also within the reach of most people nowadays and could well be useful if you misjudge the route off-road!

Piston ring compressor

These are used to clamp the new piston rings into the slots in the piston, making it easier to slide the pistons into the cylinder bore.

If you're dismantling an engine, a piston ring compressor will save a lot of hassle.

Soldering iron

Not essential, but very handy when a cable comes adrift from the rear of a light cluster or switch.

Valve spring compressor

Necessary when dismantling the cylinder head. Compressing the

A valve spring compressor will save your fingers when dismantling a cylinder head.

valve springs frees the spring collets, allowing the valves to be removed from the head.

SKILLS

The best way to gain the necessary experience is to be taught by an expert. Failing that, then books will give you a basic understanding, but really the only way to learn is to get your hands dirty. A lot of today's experts are self-taught, and even those of us who had the benefit of a vocational training will tell you that you never stop learning, and a great deal of knowledge is gained 'on the job'. So don't despair if you don't know one end of a car from the other, Suzuki 4x4s are some of the simplest vehicles to work on and, with plenty of room to manoeuvre and get at all the mechanics, you really couldn't pick a better vehicle to learn on.

Mechanics

Get yourself a workshop manual. The only difference between a novice and an experienced mechanic when it comes to workshop manuals is that experienced mechanics know that the words "gently loosen and remove ..." actually mean:

Ring edges off bolt head.
Take tops off knuckles on adjacent sharp metal thing.
Swear.
Hit repeatedly with large hammer.
Cry.
Burn off with cutting gear.
Scream, "How much?" at unsuspecting Suzuki parts attendant upon finding that the bolt you cut off is a special thread and will have to be flown in from Japan; and you appear to be paying for the whole flight.

There is no substitute for practice, just ensure you keep yourself safe. The Haynes series of books are generally pretty good at giving you relevant safety tips, so take heed of them.

Additionally join a local off-road or Suzuki 4x4 club and offer to help the guys that have the best turned out trucks. They will be only too glad of the help, and the knowledge that you will pick up will be invaluable.

Paint spraying

This title covers a multitude of topics, from a quick touch up of a rusty patch to a full respray. Either way, there are three areas that you need to get right to ensure a good paint finish: preparation, preparation, and preparation. Nothing will ruin a paint job more than sloppy rubbing down, masking up, and dusting. Although spraying itself is not as easy as it looks, 75% of the job is down to preparation.

For small areas stick to spray

cans, they are far more economical, and you're virtually guaranteed a good paint match and the paint is thinned to the correct consistency. So long as you don't load on too much paint on each pass and the conditions are okay, i.e. correct temperature and humidity, spray cans are virtually foolproof. Just don't forget to keep shaking the tin.

Bodywork repairs

I could write a whole book on panel beating, but basically if the damage is serious then it's probably cost-effective to replace the whole panel. If the damage is not too serious, then you need to get the damaged area as close as possible to its original shape, before applying thin coats of automotive filler and rubbing down with abrasive paper until a smooth, correctly-shaped finish is achieved. The finish requires rubbing down with a minimum of 400 grit wet and dry paper to obtain a sufficiently smooth finish to paint, even on an off-roader.

Bodywork is one of those areas where only practice makes perfect. By far the best way is to find an expert who will show you how. Failing that, a good instructional book will point you in the right direction. Bear in mind that I did a 5 year apprenticeship, over 20 years ago, and I'm still learning, so don't expert to master it overnight.

Welding

The most useful all round welder for automotive use is the MIG. What sets it apart from all other forms of welding is the use of an inert gas, usually part or pure argon, which shields the weld from reaction with atmospheric gases and pollution, as opposed to using a flux coated

electrode. This allows the use of wire coiled onto a motor-driven reel which provides a virtually continuous weld.

A later development saw the introduction of flux cored MIG wire, suitable for home hobby machines, which negates the need for a gas cylinder, gauge, etc. This system is more than adequate for home use, and most equipment sold, even at the lower end of the market, will have the facility to use gas if required (for stainless steel, aluminium, etc.). A 160 amp dual purpose welder

Home MIG welders are relatively inexpensive and produce perfectly acceptable welds.

is quite adequate for all welding requirements for home automotive use, including chassis repairs and

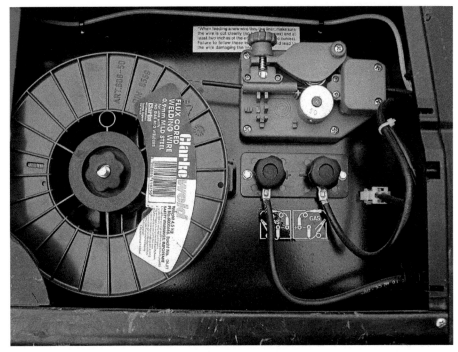

The welding wire is held on a spool and fed to the torch by motorised rollers.

construction of accessories, such as bumpers and the like.

To best appreciate how to use a MIG welder it is beneficial to understand a bit about how it works. The wire, which forms one electrode, is coiled onto a spool and fed through a pair of powered grooved rollers, which drive it up the torch liner and out of the tip. The earth clamp (the other electrode) is attached to the metal to be welded, the wire from the torch is placed next to the metal and the trigger engaged, this not only switches on the current that produces the arc (and thus the heat to form the weld) but also switches a motor that drives the wire through the torch. Once the wire is sufficiently close to the earthed material an electrical arc is formed with sufficient energy to melt steel.

In practical terms the wire reel is tensioned with a spring loaded nut, which should be tightened enough to stop the spool from unwinding, but not so tight as to prohibit the rollers from easily pulling wire from it. The rollers also have a tensioning nut to adjust their grip on the wire and for different wire diameters. The rollers are usually reversible with two groove sizes to accommodate different wire sizes.

Tensioning these two nuts, especially the latter, is important in saving time and money and reducing the frustration caused by lengthy stoppages, especially for the novice. The rollers should be tensioned so that if the arc should fail for whatever reason the rollers will not continue to feed wire through, thus saving wire and prolonging the life of the torch liner. You can dry test the tension by applying the wire to a surface, before starting to weld, and adjusting the tension accordingly.

The main controls vary the power and the speed of the wire.

Moving outside the machine, there are usually three main controls, an on/off switch, a voltage selector, which varies the power through the wire, and a wire speed regulator.

The possible variation of these controls is infinite, but basically the thinner the material the lower the power and wire speed, and vice versa. With a bit of experience you will be able to hear a good weld. It has a sort of rasping roar all of its own. This may sound strange but with a little experience you will soon understand.

Caution! – Safety equipment is essential when welding. A full-face visor, preferably a hands free model, a pair of welding gloves, and long sleeved overalls should always be worn. A hands free visor allows you to move both hands to either steady the torch or material. A visor should be used at all times. Closing your eyes will not shield them from the intense ultraviolet radiation produced during welding. The resultant arc-eye has been likened to having hot sand round the back of the eyeballs. The gloves and long sleeves will protect

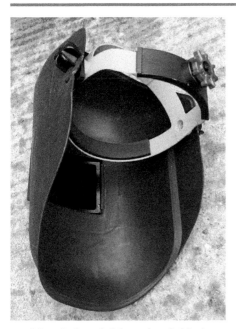

A hands-free, full-face visor is ideal.

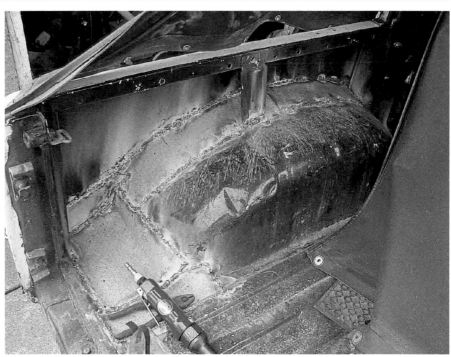

Large areas of patch repair should be tack welded in place to prevent distortion.

your skin from the ultraviolet light which can cause skin cancer. Half an hour's continuous welding can leave you with a burning sensation on any unprotected skin for a few days.

With the wire protruding about 5mm from the end of the tip and a few millimetres from the weld area, hold the gun at roughly 70 degrees to the run of the weld, pointing in the direction of the weld, with your head as close as you can to the other side of the gun to enable you to see the weld pool (the area of molten metal that forms during the welding process) and thus gauge the speed at which to move the torch. A nice steady speed will give a nice smooth weld. Too fast and you'll get the infamous 'pigeon crap', which is a line of weld along the surface with no real penetration; too slow and you risk the weld pool becoming too large to support itself, whereupon it drops out leaving a big hole.

Welding in the direction the gun is pointing means that you run

into relatively cool metal as you go, cutting your chances of producing a blow hole in thin metal. For thicker plate this can be reversed (dragging the gun) which puts the wire directly into the hottest part of the weld, increasing the weld pool and, therefore, the weld penetration. Dragging the gun also means that the area ahead of the weld run is preheated to a certain amount prior to entering the weld pool, which also increases the temperature and thus the penetration. The aim is to produce a round, even weld surface with, on thin material, disruption of the underside, indicating that full penetration has been achieved.

For long welds, such as large patches, the key is tacking. Prepare the hole to be repaired by removing all rusty steel, grind off all paint, etc., to an inch back from the edge, and cut a steel patch to overlap the hole. Then, holding the patch flush with

a piece of wood (I inevitably end up using my hammer handle) give the edge of the patch a quick blast of weld, sufficient to hold it in place. Repeat this around the edge of the patch at 3-4in intervals, starting opposite the first one to reduce the chances of distorting the patch. Once you have tack welded the patch in place you can weld all the way round. Stop at each tack and gently tap down the patch between the next two tacks so that it's flush with the metal surface to ensure a good weld. Replacing panels does not require continuous welding. Inspecting an original panel will reveal a row of spot welds. These can be imitated on the replacement by drilling or punching small holes in a similar position and then welding the panel in place by filling this hole with weld. Alternatively, small runs of weld, ¼in long every 1½in along the edge of the panel, will suffice.

Nearly all modern vehicle bodies are constructed using rows of spot welds.

A bucket of water with some soaked rags and a fire extinguisher should always be to hand when welding a vehicle.

Keep some rags in a bucket of water handy to cool the metal after welding. These also come in handy as an impromptu fire extinguisher if the paint should catch fire.

There's no substitute for practice. Cut lots of small pieces of sheet steel, 4in long for example, lay one on the other and weld them together, again and again, changing the various controls to gain experience of how they affect the weld. Try welding thicker pieces of material and, when you've mastered that, try welding thin pieces to thick pieces. Then try some T-welds and butt welds and soon you'll be able to master anything you're likely to encounter on your 4x4. Do not practice on your vehicle.

Caution! – It's important to have an assistant on hand when you're welding, to hold things for you and to keep watch for fire. A vehicle has many flammable substances, like oil, petrol, plastics, and paint, and, while you're welding inside the vehicle it's quite possible for underbody-sealant, for example, to be burning away merrily outside. It goes without saying, therefore, that a fire extinguisher is an absolute must.

DESIGN SKILLS AND IMAGINATION

Although no one can teach you imagination, you either have it or you don't, looking through magazines and websites, and even this book, should give you some inspiration to design your ideal truck. Whilst a well turned out truck will give huge amounts of pleasure, the real satisfaction is in designing and building your own thing. So by all means follow tried and tested modifications, but just make sure you give it your own edge.

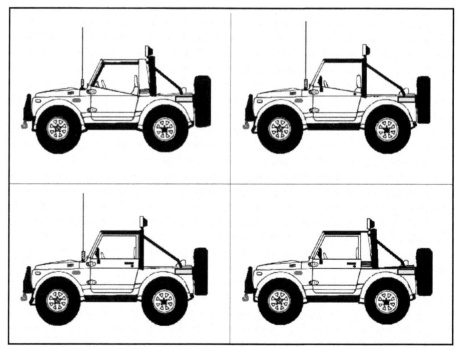

Don't be afraid to play with different designs for your pride and joy.

Chapter 4
General modifications

All the items and procedures outlined in this chapter are general to all vehicles. Significant differences between vehicles are mentioned where appropriate.

ANTI-ROLL BAR (STABILISER BAR)

Whilst on-road this is undeniably a super piece of kit that controls roll whilst cornering at speed, unfortunately, off-road, it severely limits articulation and any suspension modifications will be useless. Therefore, it has to go; in fact, you'll probably find the articulation, and thus the off-road performance, increases dramatically on even a stock truck simply by removing the anti-roll bar. **Caution!** – The handling characteristics of your truck will change dramatically following removal of the anti-roll bar, and you need to take time to get used to driving it again.

Removing the anti-roll bar may well be your first modification.

AXLE BREATHERS

The axle casings are fitted with breathers to allow the axles to vent when they become hot. Whilst this is necessary it does create a means whereby water can get into the axle housing. If the warm axle is suddenly immersed in cold water the gases inside will contract and suck in whatever is in the vicinity of

Raised axle breathers will prevent an expensive differential failure.

Wheelarches may well need some work, if not repair, then some wider arches to cover all that rubber.

the breather. If small poppet valves are fitted to the axle, this means that if they are submerged water will be sucked into the axle housing, which is not ideal.

A length of pipe can be fitted over the tubing in the axle housing that holds the poppet valve, and run up to a position high enough to avoid submerging in water. If the end of the pipe is then bent over water should not be able to gain entry to the axle and ruin the differential and wheel bearings. Conversely, the later coil sprung models which, it could be argued, are less likely to be used seriously off-road, were mostly fitted with these extension pipes, so conversion is, therefore, unnecessary.

BODYWORK

With larger tyres and, perhaps wheel spacers fitted, your vehicle will probably look like a mini monster truck. With so much rubber protruding, it's only a matter of time before you attract the attention of the police. So, if you're driving on-road, it's essential that you cover up the tyres in some fashion. There are plenty of solutions to the problem, ranging from rubber sheeting screwed to the underside of the wheelarches, and extending out to cover the tyres, to preformed custom arch extensions.

Steel trailer wheelarches cut in half lengthwise and welded over the existing wheelarches give a

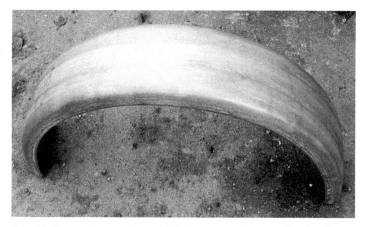

Steel trailer arches can be used to form very strong arch extensions.

good-looking, and extremely strong solution. In most cases you can get away with cutting each wheelarch in half to make two wings. This is best achieved by measuring and marking the centre line of the new arch and cutting with either a metal cutting

An inch or so of weld every few inches will give an exceedingly strong connection.

Rear disc conversion kits are best if the vehicle is to be used on the highway. (Courtesy Spidertrax)

disc in an angle grinder or a metal cutting blade in a jigsaw.

The arches will also require trimming to the correct size, which can be achieved by holding the cut arch against the existing body and marking for length. Cut the arch to size and round off any edges or sharp corners, preferably by dressing the edge over, and tack weld the arch into position. Attaching the leading edge first is preferable, then any distortion that may occur whilst straining the arch to the correct position will appear as a flow of the bodywork, whilst the front edge will remain square to the original wing. Continuous checking is the name of the game whilst fitting the opposite side, to ensure both sides align for height at the front and rear edges, and the top of the curve.

Once the arches have been satisfactorily tacked in position, permanent attachment can be

achieved by running an inch or so of weld every four inches. This, combined with the shape of the trailer arches gives an incredibly strong and rigid structure, which also adds rigidity to the original wing. With the arch extensions fitted the vehicle is transformed into a much more purposeful-looking beast.

BRAKES – REAR DISC CONVERSIONS

Drum brakes and mud do not mix, not only do they get clogged full of muck and not work effectively, but that same dirt acts as a sort of grinding paste that, if not removed, quickly reduces the shoe linings to nothing. One solution to this problem is to convert the rear brakes to discs. Discs not only reduce the loss of effectiveness from mud and dirt, they also work as well in reverse, unlike drum brakes, and they are much less hassle to service.

Caution! – Before going any further there are a few things we should get straight. Although you have the option of making your own conversion or buying a commercial kit, from Spidertrax, for example, I cannot recommend that you use the homemade conversion on the road, or indeed anywhere where you would be going more than 20mph. The other issue is that, as the rear brakes suddenly become more efficient, you will require an adjustable proportioning valve to set the brakes correctly. The stock item is not up to the job and must be replaced, again Spidertrax does a superb piece of kit.

If you are converting a Samurai, then one other issue you should bear in mind is the loss of the parking brake. This can be resolved easily

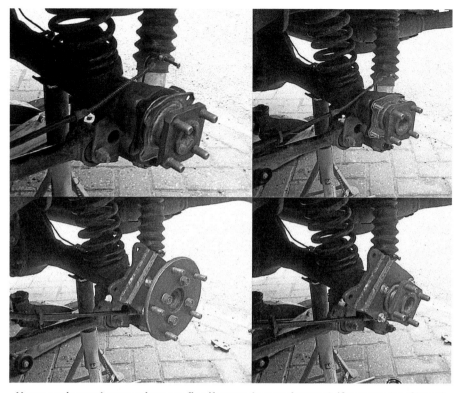

Home engineered conversions are fine if correctly manufactured. (Courtesy Jon Gilbert)

Bear in mind that the modified plate not only controls braking but also holds the wheel on. (Courtesy Jon Gilbert)

if you're fitting the SJ410 transfer box as the prop parking brake can be retained. Otherwise, a new parking/emergency brake will have to be fitted. Again, Spidertrax is the company to contact. This is covered later on.

The homemade conversion is quite complex. For a start the rear drum needs to be machined to cut down the front face to fit inside the new disc hub. As this plate will be the only thing between you and oblivion, you'd want to get it right. I've seen them cut out with a grinder; don't, you'll get to meet your maker quite soon enough without pushing your luck.

As I said the face of the drum, complete with wheel studs, needs to be machined to fit inside the new standard discs; Samurai discs, calipers and mounts are ideal. The wheel studs will need to be replaced with longer items as they'll have to protrude through the new discs which effectively shorten their length by ½in. Vitara front wheel studs are ideal.

Next, cut a square from the original drum backing plate to bolt to the end of the axle in the normal manner. This plate is then drilled to take the new caliper mounting bracket. Once this has been achieved the disc cut from the original drum face can be bolted into position on the half shaft bolts and the new brake disc positioned over it on the new wheel studs.

It is then simply a case of fitting the new callipers and pads and, once the system has been connected and bled, you are nearly ready to go. The final part of the installation is the proportioning valve, this is a fairly simple, albeit crucial and finely engineered, piece of kit. The normal brake system has a proportioning valve fitted, but this is totally useless if you have converted the rears to discs and must be replaced. Full fitting and adjustment instructions come with the kit. **Caution!** – Do not be tempted to try to get along without a new proportioning valve. I have seen different adjustments of between 70/30 and 50/50 front/rear, but it really is a case of testing the settings at different proportions, starting at low speeds and building up gradually, until you get the correct proportion to get the best from the conversion.

Fitting the manufactured kit is very similar to the above except, of course, the plate that holds the disc to the hub is supplied new and the caliper fits directly to the axle casing instead of having to cut the back plate. This is certainly the way to go if you are contemplating taking the vehicle on-road. I wouldn't like to risk my, or anyone else's, life on the strength of the cut down back plate and brake drum of the DIY conversion at any speed.

CB RADIO

CBs are very popular amongst off-roaders. When you're miles from any mobile phone signal they can be a godsend. They are no more

CB radios can be a godsend when out of mobile phone range.

difficult to fit than a standard radio, just make certain the aerial has a good earth to the bodywork or the power output and reception will be hopeless. Mount the aerial as high as possible, but if you drive through a lot of overgrown scrub this will have to be balanced with not getting it ripped off.

CLUTCH (LEAF SPRUNG VEHICLES)

One area that is easily overlooked, but which is an essential link in the transmission system, is the clutch. If you're going to be off-roading seriously and have fitted larger tyres or modified the engine to give greater power then a heavy duty or ceramic clutch is necessary. It's possible that the original diaphragm and clutch plate material will not be sufficient to handle the increases in stress and will slip even in good condition. In this case there are various replacements available. Calmini, for instance, stocks the Centraforce clutch that gives 30% increased clamping power over

standard, and the Centreforce Dual Friction clutch that has an impressive 90% improvement on the stock item. Don't expect it to be quite so easy to drive in traffic, though.

A fairly basic tool kit is all that is required to enable you to install a clutch assembly.

Firstly, for the uninitiated, I will just briefly outline the clutch components and how they work. Attached to the rear of the crankshaft is the flywheel. This serves several purposes. Firstly, it holds a certain amount of energy in the form of momentum, due to its mass, that keeps the engine running smoothly. Secondly, it has a ring gear around its outer edge that the starter pinion engages into to turn the engine over on starting, and thirdly, the clutch diaphragm is bolted to the face of the flywheel and compresses the clutch plate onto it to engage the transmission.

The clutch itself comprises a diaphragm, clutch (or driven) plate, and release bearing. The diaphragm is basically a steel shell

The clutch is a simple mechanism for disengaging power from the transmission.

enclosing the diaphragm spring, which has fingers that point into the centre. When these fingers are depressed in the centre by the release bearing, the diaphragm releases the pressure on the clutch plate, thus disengaging the clutch, and disconnecting the engine from the transmission. Normally, the full force of the diaphragm spring sandwiches the driven plate tightly enough to overcome the inertia of the transmission and wheels and imparts motion. When the driven plate wears down, the force of the diaphragm is reduced until it reaches the extremity of its movement and the clutch begins to slip even when the pedal is not depressed. The driven plate has a splined central collar that slides over the input shaft to the gearbox. Once the clutch engages this transmits power from the engine to the transmission.

To replace the clutch assembly you'll need to remove the transmission or engine. It makes sense that if you have to remove one of these items for some other reason that you replace the clutch if it's getting near its wear limit. The usual method is to remove the gearbox. I don't intend to explain this process here as it's well covered in any workshop manual. There are a few tips I will pass on, though. I have found it unnecessary to remove the exhaust so long as you are careful not to hit it and fracture the flange where it attaches to the exhaust manifold. You will need to remove the transfer box, however.

When removing the gear lever from inside the vehicle, be careful that the nylon cup on the end of the lever is removed and kept in a safe place as they have a nasty habit of dropping off into the box.

Don't let the cup from the end of the gearlever drop into the gearbox, as retrieval can be time-consuming.

Whilst either the transfer box and/or gearbox are removed the engine/gearbox will need to be supported. I usually support the gearbox on a trolley jack and the engine from above with an engine hoist. If you support the engine from below with a jack, make sure that you don't crush the sump pan as the oil pick-up is very close and any distortion may result in oil starvation.

Remove the prop shafts from the transfer case. Don't forget to mark the flanges in some way so that you re-install them in the same position. I use either a piece of white road marking crayon or a quick blast from a tin of aerosol paint. Next,

The gearbox crossmembers will need to be removed.

remove the bracket to chassis bolts, leaving the bracket attached to the transfer case, this will give you extra leverage to manoeuvre the box during removal and installation.

Now, slide the transfer case towards the rear of the vehicle and the intermediate shaft will slide from the gearbox. You may have to jack the transfer box up slightly to enable it to disconnect from the chassis before it will move. Then lower the box on the jack and remove.

Removing the gearbox is just as easy. First, though, you need to protect the distributor. Ideally, remove the distributor completely and cushion the area between the housing and the bulkhead with a piece of wood. I usually remove the distributor cap and ensure that the engine hoist is positioned so that the engine cannot move backwards far enough to damage the distributor. Be careful, though, a new distributor isn't cheap.

Whilst you are under the bonnet, remove the bolts from the starter motor and pull it clear. If you support it with some string there is no need to remove the cables, so long as you have removed the connections from the battery.

Remove the gearbox-to-crossmember nuts and bolts and lift the gearbox slightly, then remove the crossmember. Now, remove the front crossmember. You'll find the clutch release arm on the right-hand side of the gearbox, disconnect the cable and tie it up out of the way.

Finally, remove the engine to gearbox bolts and the supported gearbox should simply slide towards the rear of the vehicle. Once the input shaft is clear of the clutch assembly the gearbox can be lowered and removed from the truck.

Caution! – The dust from the wearing of the clutch plate, especially if it is an old one, may well contain asbestos. Do not inhale it. Carefully blow it out with an air-line or brush it out. Wear a mask, use an appropriate brake system cleaner and dispose of the contaminated residue and rags in a sealed, labelled container.

Now you should be able to see the clutch assembly installed on the flywheel. To remove it simply undo the bolts holding the diaphragm to the flywheel, a little at a time, alternating from one side to the other as you would tighten a set of wheel nuts, for instance. Once they are removed the driven plate can fall out so it's a good idea to support it with a clutch alignment tool whilst removing the diaphragm. Inspect the flywheel, it can be scored if the plate has worn down to rivet head level in the past and may need to be skimmed by a machine shop.

You can make a clutch alignment tool from the input shaft of an old gearbox or buy a universal kit (available from most good tool shops). All this needs to do is align the central hole with the centre of the flywheel so that when the new diaphragm is bolted on, the input

shaft will slide nicely into the centre of the driven plate. If the alignment is even slightly off-line the diaphragm won't fit. I used to make a clutch alignment tool out of a piece of dowel the right size to fit in the pilot bearing that accommodates the end of the input shaft and then winding masking tape around it in the position of the driven plate until it fitted snugly into the splined hole in the central collar. Not ideal, but it has worked admirably over the years when I haven't had the correct tool to hand.

To remove the release bearing, simply operate the release arm until the bearing is fully forward then rotate the bearing housing clockwise and it will disengage. Installation is the reverse of removal; just ensure that the pin on the release arm forks engages correctly with the slot on the release bearing.

Install the alignment tool and driven plate, ensuring the driven plate is the right way round (normally a new disc will have the appropriate side marked on it, otherwise make sure the damper coil springs in the plate are towards the gearbox) then bolt on the diaphragm and reinstall the transmission in the reverse order to removal. All that is required then is

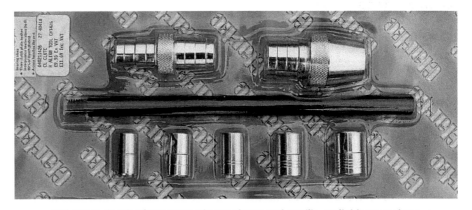

Universal clutch alignment tools are cheap and readily available nowadays.

The release bearing will usually need replacing when you fit a new clutch.

The clutch alignment tool holds the friction plate in position prior to the gearbox being re-fitted.

Off-road dampers are designed to take a huge amount of punishment.

to adjust the movement of the pedal to engage the clutch at the right position and you've finished.

DAMPERS

Dampers, or shock absorbers as they are more commonly (and incorrectly) known, serve several functions. Primarily, their role is to damp the force imparted into the springs and stop the vehicle bouncing all over the road. On a road vehicle movements are short and frequent and, as such, dampers are designed with a relatively short stroke and a reasonable resistance to the fluid's characteristics changing (i.e. foaming) whilst

Race technology is used in off-road speed event dampers.

subjected to these forces. Off-road movements can be huge and fast. The damper needs to be able to move quickly if the wheels are to keep in contact with the floor, yet still retain its damping capacity. Dampers also need far longer travel to accommodate off-road terrain.

Where longer reach is required, longer shocks are necessary. If you have lifted your suspension, then not only will you have more room for longer shocks, and thus greater articulation, but the chances are that the items that now limit the travel of your axle are your dampers at the limit of their travel. Careful damper choice is essential if the suspension modification you have lovingly fitted is to work to its best advantage. Of course, some kits will come with dampers included, otherwise consultation with one of the aftermarket damper companies will be invaluable in helping you decide on which one to choose.

All these requirements put a huge strain on the components and fluid in a damper, and it's imperative that the correct choice is made for the usage of the vehicle. For trials machines, which move slowly but require huge articulation, long travel and ease of movement are necessary: in fact, it is not unknown for trialers to have virtually no damping at all. For speed events, however, something more akin to a heavy-duty race shock is more appropriate. For general off-road use, which requires flexibility, whilst retaining good damping capabilities for on-road driving, one of the many gas filled shocks is a good bet.

DIFF LOCKER (DETROIT OR LOCK RIGHT)

However much you modify your suspension and gearing there will always be situations where a wheel loses traction. To keep you going in this situation you will require some means of transferring power to the wheel that still has traction. Probably the most cost-effective way of achieving this is the diff lock, as described in Chapter 2. (It is possible to weld the diff under certain circumstances, if the vehicle is used totally in extreme off-road conditions, for example, but I wouldn't undertake such a measure.)

Although most people will immediately think that a diff locker will go in the rear axle, there is much to be said for placing it in the front, especially if you have limited travel due to an independent front suspension, such as on the Vitara. If you're lucky enough to have an LSD fitted to the rear, which can be found on the X-ec Vitara models, then so much the better. The performance on-road will not be affected at all in two-wheel drive, and the most likely axle that will raise a wheel is the front.

Either way, fitting is fairly straightforward. You'll need to jack and support the axle in question, drain the oil and remove the half shafts. This procedure will be outlined in your workshop manual but basically involves removing the wheel, hub, brakes (including back plate) and pulling the half shaft complete from the axle; you may well need a slide hammer to achieve this. I would also strongly suggest you take the opportunity to replace the axle seals during this operation.

Once the half shafts are removed you can progress to the diff itself. The prop shaft will require removal (don't forget to mark the shaft to flange for re-fitting), then remove the diff housing bolts and remove the diff from the axle. The diff to axle seal may be fairly strong and a little upward force from a trolley jack may be required to separate the two. The jack can also be used to support the diff during removal, as it is quite heavy.

Mark the carrier bearing caps as it's imperative that the correct parts are replaced to their respective sides. Some may have a 'K' symbol, vertical on one side and horizontal on the other, with corresponding marks on the housing, but do not rely on this being the case.

Undo the four carrier retaining bolts and remove the carrier. Mark the bearings, as all parts must be rebuilt in their original positions. Then remove the ring gear to allow access to the cross-pins.

Remove the cover bolts and cover, and then remove the upper side gear. Mark the shim positions and remove for re-use. Pull out the cross-pins, the spacer, and the side gears, then clean and re-grease the carrier. Re-install the original shims

to the side gears and replace into the flanged case. Position one clutch and spacer on the side gear and install the spring caps, with the caps outward, into the slots in the clutch. Position a dowel in each of the two round holes in the clutch and repeat for the other clutch plate.

Fit the original spacer and the corresponding three cross-pins and position the second clutch. Then re-install the cap screws with their corresponding marks made during disassembly and you have the major work completed. Re-install the ring gear and put the carrier back in the housing. Then you have the task of checking the backlash and re-shimming if necessary. Torque the bearing caps and re-install the half shafts, etc. Don't forget to fill with oil, and you've finished.

Driving the vehicle may take a bit of getting used to. Firstly, if you hear clunking noises coming from the diff, especially when manoeuvring, this is normal, and is simply the teeth disengaging to allow the wheels to move differentially. Also, the truck may feel like it is being pushed in a straight line; this is because the inside wheel on a bend is, in effect, driving and the outer wheel is coasting. This can be countered to some extent by using a little throttle when cornering as opposed to letting the vehicle coast around corners. The real test will come off-road, when previously difficult terrain is traversed with ease.

ELECTRIC FAN

There are several good reasons for fitting an electric fan, including the fact that it will only cool the engine when necessary, it conserves a certain amount of engine power

The original viscous fan is fine but does sap power and can't be turned off in water.

You don't need to dismantle the pulley to remove the fan.

The fan location ties are single use devices so ensure you have positioned the new fan correctly before fitting.

(useful on the underpowered Suzuki engines), and it can be turned off when driving in deep water (which stops water being thrown all over the engine bay).

A single 10in fan is capable of cooling any of the Suzuki 4x4s up to a point. For serious off-road use it is recommended that this is doubled up with another 10in unit. Simpler by far (if room permits) is to fit a single 12in unit, which gives a 44 per cent increase over the 10in unit, and should be ample for all but the most strenuous driving in hot climates.

Fitting an electric fan is quite simple and should take no more than an hour. First, the original fan is removed by undoing the four nuts that retain the pulley. **Note!** – Don't remove the pulley itself, just the viscous fan assembly. You don't even need to remove the fan belt. At this point take the opportunity to dispose of the fan cowling on the radiator. Whilst it's fine for on-road driving, if you're driving in mud or

deep water, however, it will retain huge amounts of deposits behind the radiator, effectively halving the cooling capacity of the radiator.

Once the fan has been removed and the nuts re-installed, the new fan and housing can be installed. There are several means of attaching the fan unit to the radiator but a common and simple method employs plastic ties that fit through the radiator core and are held in place with a kind of speed nut. Do not over-tighten these ties as you can strip the teeth off them and they will no longer tighten.

Next, fit the thermostat housing near to the radiator top hose. If you have a Samurai and have removed the air filter housing to fit a snorkel there will be no shortage of space to mount it. If not, then anywhere near enough for the thermostat bulb to reach the top hose will be okay. The copper bulb must then be placed inside the top hose where it fits onto the radiator. A special rubber seal,

which houses the copper pipe, is commonly supplied. These quite often leak at first but with a little adjustment and tightening they usually settle down.

The power lead is then connected to the positive battery terminal and the other end to the fan connector. The fan earth lead goes to one side of the thermostat and the other thermostat lead goes to a good earth. It is then only necessary to adjust the thermostat. **Caution!** – Don't be tempted to set the fan thermostat too low, or it will negate the cooling system thermostat and the engine will run cool, with the fan permanently switched on.

If it's likely that the fan and thermostat are going to be used in deep water, a fan with a sealed motor and thermostat should be sourced. Many electric fan kits are referred to as 'Off-Road' but not many supply a sealed thermostat. If an ordinary unit is used it will quickly become blocked with mud, corrode from all the water contact, and generally fall apart. Some even have cardboard insulation, but these don't tend to last long at all.

Correctly installed, an electric fan can be a great advantage.

actual Phillips groove is quite small in relation to it. The only advice I can give you is make sure you have exactly the right sized Phillips bit for the screw head and use either a T-bar screwdriver or a ratchet set and screwdriver attachments. This will hopefully give you the necessary torque without destroying the soft metal of the screw head. If all this fails sawing a cross groove across the head along one of the planes of the Phillips grooves may allow you to undo it with a large flat-bladed screwdriver.

I like to manoeuvre the lump using the manifolds, when it's dangling in the air, so I leave them on. Just undo the bolts that hold the exhaust flange to the manifold and let it hang down; it won't come to any harm.

Remove the radiator cap and drain the coolant from the tap found at the right-hand bottom

ENGINE REMOVAL

This can be a very daunting prospect for novices, but so long as you are careful there is nothing a novice can't tackle. Whilst on the subject of being careful, be extra careful that any lifting gear, etc., is in good condition, is designed for the job, and that you know how to operate it before you start using it.

I have my own routine which I shall outline here. It may not be textbook but it's certainly time efficient, which is the main thing. The first step is to disconnect the battery. Label up the HT leads and unplug them all from the spark plugs, and disconnect the coil lead from the coil. Next, undo the clips on the distributor, remove the cap, and put the whole 'spider' in a safe place. Take off the rotor arm and put it with the leads and cap.

Label the coil wires, disconnect them, and remove the coil. The coil

screws can be extremely tight and, although they have big heads, the

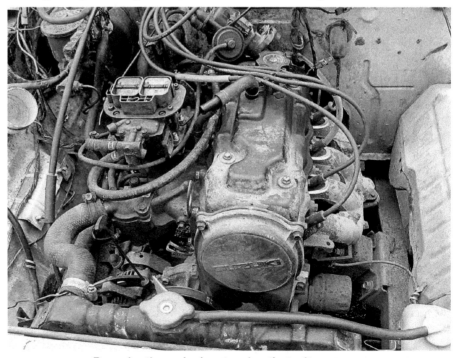

Removing the engine is not as daunting as it may seem.

Drain the coolant by unscrewing the radiator drain plug.

end of the radiator, as viewed from the front. Once all the coolant has drained, undo the top and bottom hoses where they fit to the engine. Leaving them attached to the radiator ensures they are in the correct position on replacement, have not been disturbed (which might cause leaking), and saves you time messing about unduly with inaccessible hose clips. You may wish to take the opportunity to replace the hoses, but they are easier to replace once the radiator has been removed.

Now you need to undo the bolts holding the fan and pulley assembly to the water pump. There's no need to remove the pulley or fan belt, and you can replace the screws finger tight to keep the pulley in place. Once the fan is out of the way you can remove the screws that hold the radiator mount to the uprights and lift the radiator clear. Removing the fan also ensures you don't stick it through the radiator at this juncture.

With the radiator out of the way you should feel like you're getting somewhere. Now remove all the wires from the alternator and tie them up out of the way.

Then take the cables off the starter motor solenoid and tie them out of the way too. There's no necessity to remove any of the ancillary items yet, although the starter motor will require removal prior to disconnecting the engine from the gearbox. If you wish to remove them and replace them on a new engine, take them off after you've removed the whole unit from the engine bay. There's more than enough room in an SJ engine bay to leave them attached and not damage them on extraction or installation.

Remove the air box from the top of the carb, the fuel supply and return pipes, manifold heater pipes, and the fuel cut-off solenoid lead. Release the throttle cable by pulling open the throttle by hand, which allows enough slack in the cable to line it up with the slot in its holder, and pop the nipple out. Then simply undo the nuts on either side of the

cable bracket that holds the cable in place, remove and tie up safely. If you have a choke cable fitted remove that as well. If you have an auto-choke you won't need to worry. Now remove the four bolts which hold the carburettor to the manifold and remove it.

There should be lifting rings already fitted to the front of the inlet manifold and the rear of the exhaust manifold. The lifting chains/hooks need to be fitted through these, rather than wrapped round the engine. The lifting eyes give you a well-balanced load when the engine is hanging free, which is especially helpful when it comes to replacing the unit.

Once the hoist is in place take up the slack and turn your attention to the rear of the engine. Here you'll find a variety of nuts and bolts that attach the block to the bell housing, including the two that secure the

With the engine supported by the hoist, it can be prised away from the gearbox.

Remove the engine mounts from the chassis rails.

starter motor. These all need to be removed, some from under the vehicle. There may or may not be a half plate that blocks the bottom of the bell housing, and this can be removed from below.

Once you're certain all connections have been severed with the engine you can remove the engine mount bolts. Leave the mounts on the engine and remove them from the chassis. It's much easier to realign the mounts on the chassis where you can see the holes

when it comes to re-installation.

Place a trolley jack beneath the gearbox to support it, this will allow the engine to move in and out more freely. Take the weight of the engine on the hoist, grasp the manifolds in both hands and heave the engine towards the front of the vehicle. If you can't rock the engine away from the bell housing at this point you may have left something attached, so double check. Be careful, though, because the engine can suddenly loosen and swing forward. Once the engine is free you can jack it clear of the engine bay.

FIRE EXTINGUISHER

Hopefully you will never require this piece of kit, but to go off-road without one is madness. For a small outlay you can purchase one, and preferably two, 1kg powder extinguishers and fit them within reach of the driver's seat, so that they are accessible in an emergency. Unless you are in some form of

speed event, in which case there will almost certainly be strict regulations as to what is required, this should be ample for most eventualities.

HARNESSES

Harnesses are not imperative for recreational off-roading, a good set of seat belts will protect you admirably in most cases. However, if you're venturing over serious terrain, then harnesses should be on your list of things to fit. Not only do they keep you safe during an accident, but they also hold you securely in your seat when manoeuvring off-road, which can be very useful. There are varying standards of manufacture and specifications, such as strap widths, etc., but for recreational off-road use, a Clubman-style three-point harness should be sufficient.

Always carry a fire extinguisher in your vehicle.

Harnesses give far more support in the event of an accident and should be considered essential for off-road use.

Once the engine is free, it can be lifted clear of the engine bay.

A simple three- or four-point harness (points simply being the number of fixings to the vehicle) should be ample unless you are envisaging driving like a madman. They consist of two side straps that usually fit to the existing seat belt mounts, via screw in eye bolts, and two over-the-shoulder belts, that either join behind the neck to become one belt in a three-point harness, or bolt into two separate mounts in a four-point setup. If you want to be really secure then there are also five- and six-point harnesses, both of which have the upper straps of the four-point and either one or two additional crotch straps, which make up the additional securing points.

HYDRAULIC HANDBRAKE

Before reading this you should be aware that I am reasonably certain that an inline hydraulic lock is illegal for road use, at least in the UK, so if you're going on-road this system will need to be supplemented with an additional mechanical handbrake.

If fitting a rear disc brake conversion, the handbrake setup can be a problem. Fitting a fully functional handbrake assembly is an expensive undertaking, and fitting the old SJ prop shaft parking brake is not necessarily the best option, although it does lock all four wheels when in four-wheel drive, which can be a lifesaver off-road, and is a good way of keeping within Construction and Use Regulations.

If you do require an hydraulic setup, then an inexpensive alternative is the Jamar inline hydraulic lock, which is operated by pushing down on the brake pedal and depressing the parking brake

A Jamar inline hydraulic lock can be used as an hydraulic handbrake off-road. (Courtesy Spidertrax)

lock. Basically, you are pressurising the system with the foot pedal and sealing the pressure to the rear brakes with the valve. To release the brake you simply release the park lock while pushing down on the brake pedal.

INSTRUMENTS

Many additional instruments can be fitted; some useful, such as a voltmeter and ammeter, especially if you're running a winch; and some not so useful, such as pitch and inclinometers. I once described these as only being useful for

hanging on to when you roll over and I haven't changed my opinion. If you're at an angle where you need to check it on a gauge then the last thing you should be looking at is the dashboard.

An oil pressure gauge is also a useful addition and not difficult to fit, especially the pressurised variety, which has a take-off plate that fits between the oil filter and its housing. Probably more useful is a large oil pressure warning light. I have a dash-mounted Samurai indicator side repeater lamp wired up. This gives ample warning should the oil pressure suddenly drop, and the engine can be turned off immediately before any serious damage occurs.

LONG SHACKLES

Long shackles are the simplest and cheapest form of suspension modification. To raise the chassis one inch above the axle you'll need to lengthen the shackles by two inches. This is due to the leaf spring being hinged at one end, so, to increase the distance travelled halfway along its length (i.e. the position of the axle) you need to increase the distance at the end of the spring by twice the amount.

There are some good long shackles available, or it is quite

Inclinometers and the like make nice ornaments but are practically useless.

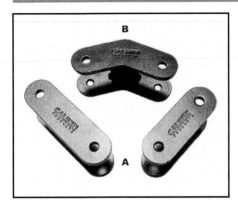

Increased length shackles are fine if well made and limited to 4in longer than standard. (Courtesy Calmini)

possible to make your own. For a simple one inch lift, each shackle will require two pieces of steel bar, two inches longer than the original shackle at the bolts, with appropriate holes drilled in them. Any further height will require some form of welded cross-bracing and, in any case, I would not condone any more than a two inch lifting shackle (i.e. four inches longer than standard) even for entirely off-road applications.

PROP SPACERS
If you significantly raise the suspension, you will need to investigate the propshafts. Increasing the distance between axle and chassis also increases the distance between axle and transfer box. Combine this with increased articulation and the length of the splined section on the props, which takes up the movement of the suspension, is soon used up. At extreme articulation this can mean the prop simply falls out, which is embarrassing at best. To combat this you can either fit custom prop shafts with elongated splined areas, or fit a spacer between the prop and axle flanges to take up some of the slack.

Prop spacers take up the extra length between the transfer box and differentials following suspension lifts. (Courtesy Calmini)

Spacers are usually constructed of billet aluminium, pre-drilled to take longer flange bolts and machined to fit the flange faces. These come in various lengths from ½in to 1½in to fit different severities of suspension modification. Much greater than this and you'll need custom built prop shafts.

RADIATOR
One area where all the Suzuki 4x4s fall down is the radiator. If used in deep muddy water the radiator core will swiftly fill with mud, which, once taken out of the water, quickly dries and sets. It's almost impossible to remove once it has gotten to this stage. Unfortunately, due to the speeds encountered driving off-road it's probable you will notice nothing untoward until you are driving

home at highway speeds. Don't be tempted to try and wash the mud out with a pressure washer; the force of the water is more than sufficient to crush the foil fins in the radiator core rendering it totally useless. If your radiator gets to this condition the only hope is to remove it and soak it in a caustic solution. Of course this will not get you home from the off-road centre.

You can move the radiator to the rear of the vehicle but this can have its own problems with lack of airflow and pump capacity for all that extra pipework. A gauze panel across the front of the radiator prior to immersion can work well, but if it's not removed and cleaned immediately afterwards it can also block the airflow and cause overheating.

REMOVABLE DOORS (HINGE MODIFICATION)

With the external design of the hinges this is a simple process. One way or another you must cut off the top section of the hinge fitted to the wing. This enables the door to simply be lifted off the hinge pin. You can make the cut with an angle grinder, but you can also use a Dremel, or something similar.

Once you've removed the top section you'll need to cut the hinge pin just about flush with the top

only snag is the door check strap that will need to be removed and replaced every time you swap doors. Do not be tempted to run without them; open the doors with a slight breeze or on a slope and they will swing forward and crease, not only themselves, but the front wings as well. There are quick release straps on the market, but it's possible to make a set yourself from a couple of old sports bag straps or the like, that use the large quick release catches.

behind the seats, strutted to the rear arches or floor may not save your truck, but it will probably save you. A front section with legs down the door pillars to the front floor and braced below the roof will be more likely to ensure your survival. If you use all four seats off-road then you will require a rear section as well.

If you think as much of your truck as you do of yourself then an external cage may save it from being trashed during a roll. I just don't like the look of them, but it is undeniable that a good external cage will be worth its weight in gold when a large investment of your time and cash is rolling sideways down a hill.

There are many designs on the market and it is not beyond the scope of a competent engineer to build a cage in the home workshop. However, for various reasons, I shall not be covering the build here.

Cut down hinges allow the doors to be removed for additional flexibility.

of the centre section of the hinge to enable it to come off the pin when lifted. Then simply round off the top of the pin to facilitate easy replacement and tidy up the top section of hinge where it's been cut.

Do a good job, give it a good coat of paint and people hardly notice the difference. The bottom of the hinge is perfectly strong enough to support the weight of the door and, for those security conscious ones amongst you, it's impossible to lift the doors off without having them fully open first so there is very little reduction to security.

There is, however, a great deal more flexibility in your truck. The

ROLL CAGE

A roll gage is probably *the* most important safety item off-road. The chances are if you off-road long enough, eventually you will roll your truck. The upper half of a Samurai is not strong, especially a soft top; that roll hoop will not support the weight of the truck. It does not have to be a 50mph roll, just a gentle drop down a 4 foot slope can be enough to end your off-road career, permanently. It is likely that nine times out of ten you will simply land the truck on its side, shake yourself off and admire the bent roof, but is it worth the risk?

Cages come in stages, in a two-seater a simple internal roll hoop

An internal roll cage might just save your life ... (Courtesy Calmini)

... an external one may save your truck as well.

ROOF RACKS

A very handy piece of kit; all manner of bits and pieces can be stored here, including spare wheels. Just remember the more weight you put up there the higher the centre of gravity becomes.

A roof rack may be very useful but beware of raising the centre of gravity too high. (Courtesy Calmini)

SEATS

For most purposes the original seats are fine, and it's really a matter of personal preference whether to replace them or not. Granted, a nicely fitted sports seat will give you far more stability, but for anything less than competition use it's debatable whether it's necessary. For a cheaper alternative, especially if the originals have completely had it, second-hand seats from a sports saloon car are a popular swap, although it should be noted that, due to the differing carrier dimensions, this is not a simple bolt in job.

Whatever the choice of seat, something that they all benefit from is a waterproof cover. These are available in different styles from virtually any motor accessory store and are well worth the investment. The pleasure derived from being able to simply throw the seat covers in the washing machine, rather than facing the daunting task of trying to dry and clean mud soaked cloth seats is immense. They bring the additional advantage of ensuring the longevity of your seats and, for the price, are a very worthwhile investment.

SKID PLATES

Skid plates can be fitted to any of the vulnerable under-body components, such as the diff housings, engine sump, transfer box, steering rods and axles. Made of anything from aluminium to galvanised steel, skid plates protect the expensive bits of your truck from damage from rocks and tree stumps. If you're only going to fit one sort, fit some diff housing covers. The plates on the rear of the diff housings are not particularly strong, and contact with any heavy obstacle can push the diff housing against the ring gear which can, in turn, form a pretty good grinder and cut right through the plate exposing the diff to the elements.

SNORKEL

If you intend to take your vehicle anywhere near water then an

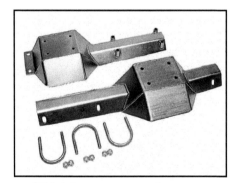

Skid plates can save you from some expensive and embarrassing failures. (Courtesy Calmini)

elevated air intake should be high on your list of modifications. In basic form, a snorkel is simply a tube connected to the vehicle's air intake that raises its height above that where water could reasonably be expected to reach. Normally this is around the area of the roofline in front of the windscreen. If the water has reached this level then getting it in your engine is likely to be the least of your worries.

The problem with water is it does not lend itself to being compressed to the same degree as air. If you wish to experiment with this phenomena then take a simple bicycle pump and pull it fully back, then place your finger over the hole and push the handle down, making note of how far you can push it in. Now repeat the experiment, but this time before you pull back the pump immerse the hole in water and fill the pump up. Now try and compress it with your finger over the hole again. Impressive isn't it?

Now try to imagine what happens to the internals of your engine if you suck water into the air intake when it attempts to compress it to a ninth of its normal volume, it's not pretty. Bent and broken connecting rods are usually the first casualty, but all sorts of other nasties can occur. Suffice it to say repairs will not be cheap.

There are various snorkels on the market, but for the budget conscious, or those who simply don't wish to see a reasonably significant investment flattened or torn off by a passing tree there is another alternative. Plastic rainwater goods are a simple, cheap and readily available means of constructing a snorkel that is perfectly adequate, can be made to look reasonably professional, and doesn't cost a small fortune to replace should it get damaged off-road.

If you're going anywhere near deep water, a snorkel is an absolute must.

A homemade snorkel will not reduce you to tears when it gets ripped off.

As with all these things there has to be a drawback, and the main one with fitting a snorkel is finding the courage to take a drill to your pride and joy's wing. As the hole has to be the exact diameter of the pipe, in the right place and precisely circular, it can all be a bit daunting.

On the Vitara/Sidekick in the rear of the nearside inner wing there is a hole where the air intake pipe from your filter housing disappears. This is also where your new pipe will enter the engine bay. Providentially the hole is exactly the same diameter as the external diameter of 68mm PVC pipe. When I say the fit is exact, I mean exact, it may well take a bit of fiddling and pushing before you get the pipe through, but it fits perfectly and holds the pipe steady.

To access this hole you will need to undo the pipe from the filter housing. This leaves you with a short protruding pipe, which is part of the plastic intake housing bolted between the outer and inner wings. You will have to remove the plastic wheelarch insert to get at it, but it's fairly easy, being held in with a few screws in plastic mounts in the wings. Once removed, you can see the air intake, a long, rectangular, black plastic box. The steel straps holding this is in place bolt through the inner wing near the top. Undo the small nuts on the inner wing and it will fall out.

Cut a short length of downpipe and force it through the inner wing until it touches the outer wing, this will give you a target for the drill. You may at this point be contemplating using a hole saw to cut the hole in one go. However, due to the curve in the wing, right where you want to drill, and the chances of actually getting it in the correct spot first time, I would seriously not recommend it.

Instead, invest in a drill file and round and half-round files. With the pipe protruding into the engine bay it is relatively easy to line up a pencil on the outer wing roughly in the centre of the pipe. Put a mark there and bore a hole. Now you can see into the pipe and gauge its position. Making sure the pipe is pushed up against the inside of the outer wing and is straight in both planes, drill a ring of small holes, quite close together, through the wing, so that they are all just inside the pipe. You don't want to make a mistake here or it will cost you a new wing, so be careful. Insert a drill file through one of the holes and file away the remaining metal between the holes, until the centre piece falls out and you have one big hole. It's a good idea to use a variable speed drill to achieve this, as the file can be a bit aggressive on thin sheet steel. It's also possible with a metal cutting blade in a jigsaw but, due to the

thinness of the sheet, it can be a bit difficult to control.

Next, using the pipe as a guide, file the top of the hole to the correct size and shape, gradually pushing the pipe through as the hole progresses through the top curve of the wing. Once the pipe is flush with the flatter, bottom part of the wing, use the pipe as a guide to file the bottom half of the hole to shape. The neater the hole, the more professional the installation will appear. Once it's all installed a bead of silica sealant round the pipe on both sides of the wing will keep the rust at bay and finish it off nicely.

For a Vitara, you'll need a length of downpipe, one right angle bend, two obtuse angles, one wall mount and a flat end plate. Some form of sealant, preferably one that also holds fast, will also be required to hold the construction together.

With these it is possible to get the correct angles to run the pipe up the screen pillar and leave a flat base for the air filter. This might sound simple, but once you start putting things together you'll realise just how fortuitous it is that the angles of the bends are exactly the same as that of the screen pillar. Place the 90 degree bend on the end of the pipe through the wing and push the pipe in as far as it will go. Then push the bend flush with the wing and put one of the obtuse bends into the right angle bend. As the obtuse angle fits inside the pipe diameter and the right angle bend fits outside, you'll need to cut a piece of downpipe as a spacer to fit these two together. Sadly, on the SJ body shape the angles are not correct to enable a neat fitting. However, a spare carb to air filter box ribbed hose makes an excellent elbow joint.

Now all you have to do to finish the outside is fix the wall mount to the screen pillar. I found that, with the combination of tight fitting holes and the adhesive in the pipe joints, it's only necessary to fit one near the top of the pipe to hold it very firmly indeed.

Using the other obtuse angle you need to decide what height you want the filter, around roof level looks good. Cut your pipe to the right length, pop in the bend, put the flat end plate on top and adjust the angle until it's parallel to the roof line and you have a mounting face for the filter. Then, simply bolt a filter to the top to keep the muck out and you are finished. It looks pretty neat and is virtually maintenance free.

On the Vitara, you can use the existing air filter housing. Take out the filter element, though, as you already have a filter atop the snorkel, and prise out the section containing the warm air thermostat, which, unless you want to draw water up it, has to go. Remove the thermostat and the flap and blank off and seal both holes and replace the section into the filter housing. The existing flexible pipe should be sufficient to connect the housing to the pipe, although they do perish badly, so check. For the SJ/Samurai you simply need to fit the ribbed rubber pipe from the filter box to the new snorkel.

On the SJ/Samurai you have a choice of which wing you wish the snorkel to go through. If you're likely to be fitting a winch, and, therefore, a second battery, it's preferable to fit the snorkel to the wing with the existing battery to prevent any later positioning problems. Also, the bend that takes the pipe up the screen pillar is better replaced with a length

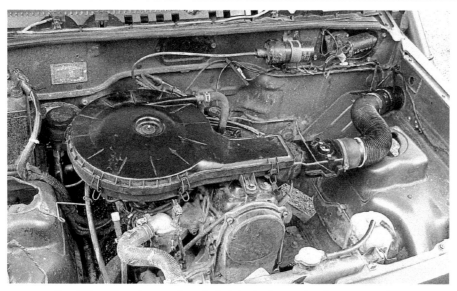

On a Vitara there is a readymade hole in the inner wing for your snorkel.

Samurai snorkels are best cut into the bonnet, especially if larger wheelarches and additional batteries are to be fitted.

of corrugated rubber hose, such as that (from a scrap vehicle) which goes between the air filter housing and the airbox atop the carburettor.

The pipe length in the engine bay will either have to reach across to the existing rubber hose that fits to the carburettor intake or a series of pipes and hoses can be made to fit, just ensure they are airtight. Don't use ordinary tubing; reinforced tubing, such as that already fitted, is necessary or the pipe will collapse under the suction from the carburettor at high throttle velocity. One benefit is that the wings are flat and easier to mark and cut than the Vitara/Sidekick, although, if you're going to fit larger wheelarches at a later date you must bear that in mind at the marking out stage.

A final check to ensure all the vacuum and breather hoses are connected correctly to the intake system, and replace any perished or split items, and the job is complete.

SPOTLIGHTS

Fitting the lights is straightforward, but the wiring is not quite as easy as it might be as the system is earth switched (i.e. the switch is on the earth, rather than the power side of the lights). The accompanying diagram shows how to wire in two sets of spots with the relay permanently live so that it trips when the headlamp wire goes to earth. It's not difficult, just a pain.

When the switch is in the top position the roof spots are switched with high beam, in the middle position they are permanently off and in the lower position they are permanently on. The bull bar spots always come on with the high beam, though. The blue wire, the high beam wire, is normally positive when high

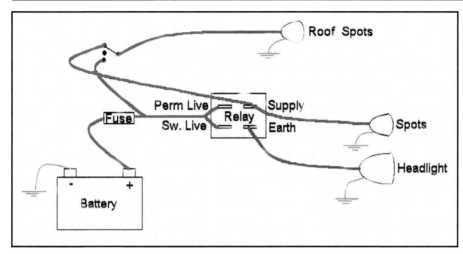

Spotlights are not as simple to wire in as they might be due to the lights being switched on the earth side of the circuit. (Courtesy Dave Jones)

beam is off, but reverses to negative when high beam is on. This in turn gives the relay an earth and switches the power through to the spots, hence the 'switched' live is actually a permanent live, rather than the relay 'trigger'. (Don't forget to fuse both of them).

STARTER RELAY

You jump in your truck, turn the starter and; click, click, click, click. If this is familiar, especially with a warm engine, then you need to fit a relay into your starter circuit. Particularly on SJs the starter circuit via the ignition switch is just simply not up to the job. A 20 amp continuous, 30 amp maximum rated relay will remedy the situation. Most relays are numbered the same so, connect terminal 87 to the male spade connector on the starter motor, terminal 30 to the positive battery post, terminal 86 to the ignition switch lead removed from the starter terminal, and 85 to earth. All you are doing is energising the relay with the ignition switch circuit, which throws the relay, connecting the battery direct to the starter.

SUMP BAFFLES

Due to the steep terrain encountered off-road, engine oil can be suddenly slopped into the front or rear of the sump, exposing the oil pick up and losing oil supply. This is particularly likely if the oil level is not maintained at maximum. To counter this effect small plates can be welded to the inside of the sump pan to restrict the flow of oil when the engine is inclined. The plates should run transversely across the sump pan and have a hollow beneath them that allows some movement of oil in the sump, and should obviously not be in a position where there is likely to be contact with any moving parts. They are not intended to stop movement of oil in the sump merely to slow it down so that sudden inclines do not starve the engine of oil just when it is likely to be under most stress.

SWING-AWAY TYRE RACKS

Excellent for saving those rear door hinges when you have huge tyres fitted and imperative if your spare will no longer fit above the bumper. They can also be adapted to carry farm jacks and the like.

Swing-away tyre carriers allow much bigger tyres to be carried and relieve the strain on the rear door. (Courtesy Calmini)

Fitting larger tyres requires a variety of modifications to suspension and gearing.

TYRES

There is little to be gained by fitting huge aggressive tyres to a vehicle and then either not having sufficient power to use them or breaking transmission components because of them. It is reasonable to suggest that choice of tyre size is the major determining factor in the type of suspension modification required. Put simply, if you wish to drive off-road then theoretically the higher your axles are above any obstacle

the better. However, this must be tempered by the stability of the vehicle, its power and the owner's budget.

The accompanying table outlines the common choices of tyre and the appropriate suspension and vehicle modifications for the SJ413/Samurai.

The European and US nomenclature need not be daunting. In the American style the first number is the overall diameter,

followed by width and finally wheel size. For example 31x10.50x15 is 31in overall diameter, 10.50 tyre width on a 15in diameter wheel rim. This is very helpful for the modifier, as all the necessary information is available at a glance.

The European sizes require a certain amount of working out to gain similar information. A typical tyre might be a 255/80/15. This relates to tyre width in millimetres/profile percentage/wheel diameter. A simple equation can be employed to convert this into a reasonably accurate US comparable size. For our purposes, the letter speed rating will be ignored, as it's doubtful the vehicle will attain even the lowest speed limit.

Dividing the width in mm by 25.4 will give the tyre width in inches:

255/25.4 = 10.04 (nominally 10in)

Multiplying this figure by the percentage profile will give the tyre height:

10 x 0.8 = 8

To calculate the overall tyre diameter, it is necessary to double the tyre height and add the wheel diameter:

(8 x 2) + 15 = 31

Giving a comparable tyre size of:

31 x 10 x 15

Generally speaking, tyres need to be as aggressive as necessary. There is no point fitting hugely

Suspension	Tyre size	Body mod	Transmission
Stock	27in	None	Stock
1.5in	29in	None	Stock
2in	30in	Slight	Baby Lobster
Stock	31in	Major	Baby Lobster
3in	31in	Slight	Baby Lobster
4in	32in	Slight	Rock Lobster
5in	33in	Minor	Rock Lobster
5in	35in	Major	Vitara diffs

Treads need to be as aggressive as the terrain demands.

get scratched and corroded with the abuse they get off-road, and if they receive a severe impact they can break. A steel wheel may bend, but in an emergency it can usually be bent back into shape with a hammer; at least enough to enable you to reach civilisation.

The offset on the different wheels means that Samurai wheels are an advantage on a Vitara, but not vice versa. The 16in wheels from a Grand Vitara also have the same stud pattern and allow the fitment of a whole new range of tyre sizes, previously denied the average Suzuki owner.

WHEEL SPACERS

One of the best ways of overcoming the problem of tyres fouling the front leaf springs and bodywork

aggressive tractor tyres if you only drive the odd lane occasionally and 95% of your driving is on-road. By the same token, you'll not get far with All Terrain tyres at an off-road centre. If you predominantly run on-road but want good off-road performance you really have little option than to either have two sets of tyres or run mud tyres on the road. Most off-road sites nowadays will not allow tyres any more aggressive than road legal Mud Terrains and it's unlikely that there is any terrain there that would warrant anything more. For trials events, etc., dumper tyres are usually de rigour.

WHEELS

There are hundreds of wheel styles to choose from, just ensure you have the correct size wheel for the tyres you are fitting; any wheel or tyre stockist will be able to advise you. You cannot fit 31in tyres on standard rims, for example.

Be aware that, although alloy wheels look great, they are likely to

Alloy wheels might look great when clean but I doubt if the driver of this diesel-engined, 33in Simex-tyred SJ worries too much that.

is to fit wheel spacers. This gives the additional benefits of widening the track of the vehicle (improving stability) and lessens the turning circle by way of allowing greater turn in before fouling the bodywork or springs, which is obviously more noticeable on a leaf sprung vehicle.

There are some bulletproof looking bits of kit on the market, with billet spacers containing holes for the existing studs, countersunk to take the nuts, and complete with new studs installed in the spacer itself. These look very nice, and are virtually indestructible, but the price can be a bit prohibitive.

Another design, sold by Grayston in the UK, consists of a set of elongated bolts and a hollow aluminium spacer. Fitting is a fairly straightforward process, albeit a little bit fiddly, as the wheel stud extensions have to be torqued up on the studs, but must also fit in the hexagonal holes in the spacer to prevent them coming undone in use. This may sound easy, but the chances of getting the nut in the right place at the right torque is unlikely, to say the least, so a bit of judicious fiddling is required to line them all up.

Once all the nuts are aligned the spacer simply slips over the top, with the studs protruding through the aforementioned holes. Then you can simply position the wheel over the extended studs and put on the wheel nuts in the normal manner.

The wheel stud extensions can be difficult to align, but it's by no means onerous. The one piece of advice I would give you is ensure that they line up perfectly with the holes in the spacers by trying them again and again until the spacer simply slides over the studs. It may

Wheel spacers will be necessary with large tyres to prevent fouling leaf springs and bodywork.

The wheel studs are elongated by fitting extension nuts.

be quicker to tap them in place with a hammer if they don't quite fit, but it will be more time consuming in the long run when they start to come loose!

The other problem is keeping the spacer in place whilst fitting the wheel, as the spacer is held in place by the wheel nuts. Once fitted, you will almost certainly require some wheelarch extensions if you are driving on the highway, especially if you are fitting wider tyres as well.

Note! – There has been a fair amount of discussion about the

The aluminium spacer not only seats the wheel but also locks the extension nuts in position.

safety of wheel spacers recently in the UK Suzuki fraternity as there have been a few accidents where spacer studs have sheared off leaving the driver with a three-wheeled truck. I have seen no evidence to suggest there is anything inherently wrong with the spacers themselves and suspect that it is more a result of incorrect fitment and lack of maintenance.

WINCHES
It's a fact that, not long after you venture off-road, you will get stuck. There is an old adage in the off-road fraternity that if you don't get stuck you aren't trying hard enough, and there is a lot of truth in that. The more experienced you become the harder you will push your machine, to its limits and beyond. Indeed, the only way to find the limitations of yourself and your vehicle is to attempt to push beyond them. Eventually, you may decide that some form of self-retrieval is necessary, but be warned, once you have a winch it is unlikely it will just be used for self-recovery; you may suddenly become the most popular guy on an event!

A powerful winch will prove a great investment. (Courtesy KAP Suzuki)

A good quality winch will last for many years if regularly serviced.

On the face of it, it may appear that a vehicle as light as a Samurai can be pulled by a winch with a 2000lb rating. There are many reasons why this is not the case. Firstly, the rating of the winch is given at its most efficient. With several turns of cable on the drum this will be significantly reduced. Also, a vehicle on a flat hard road is different to one stuck up to its axles

in a quagmire of clay. Even if the winch manages to pull the vehicle free, its components, especially the motor, will be severely strained.

For these reasons alone a rating of 6000lb should be regarded as nominal. If you are likely to use your winch on more than an occasional basis you may want to consider having a twin battery setup. Many people will tell you that it is imperative that you have a dual charging system, but this is not the case. A simple parallel connection to the new battery will suffice, although a high output alternator would be very welcome. It can be a good idea to put an isolation switch in the positive connection to the new battery so that under extreme winching you can effectively

disconnect the new battery and save some charge to ensure you have enough battery power left to run the vehicle afterwards.

WINCH BUMPERS
The stock bumper is not up to taking a winch and the associated stresses so you'll need a replacement bumper. You can build your own, of course, but you'd need to be very confident of your welding abilities. A winch bumper should be first and foremost inherently strong; a good one will also be stylish and increase the vehicle's approach angle.

Don't be tempted to simply bolt the bumper through the four inner chassis rail end holes, though, as these have been known to rip through. It's a much better idea to bolt right through the chassis rail, with a tubular spacer over the bolts between the sides of the rail. Better yet, reinforce the front chassis cross-rail by fitting a suitable diameter steel tube within it, and an additional clamp around it as part of the bumper design. The bumper end irons will have to be removed but this will also increase tyre clearance.

A good winch bumper will be strong, light and stylish, and will also increase the approach angle.

Chapter 5
Leaf sprung vehicles

LJ80

Probably the oldest of the Suzuki four-wheel drives you are likely to come across, certainly in the UK, in any condition worthy of modification is the LJ80. At first glance this may not seem a viable option for an off-road machine, but rest assured there are some extremely good versions of this little 4x4 still going strong. In standard guise it is undoubtedly painfully slow as far as highway travel is concerned, but there have been various power plant transplants into this baby of the Suzuki family, including the popular 1600 8-valve Vitara engine, 1300 SJ/Samurai engine, 1300 Geo Metro engine and gearbox, and even V6 and V8 power plants.

It would be misleading to suggest that any of these swaps are easy options, however. None of the above units swap straight into the vehicle, and it is necessary

A well-prepared 1.6-litre Vitara-engined LJ80.

to trash nearly all the transmission and suspension in most cases, and usually seriously modify the body in the areas of the bulkhead and transmission tunnel as well.

At the time of writing, I know of no mainstream modification kits available for the LJ. It is undeniable that the little truck has an appeal all of its own, however, and there

There are plenty of LJ80s still going strong. (Courtesy Sarg)

are many devoted fans across the world. There are even some serious off-road versions of the older models, such as the LJ10. Sadly, however, as they could not be called a mainstream machine, this is all the coverage of the LJ marques there is room for in this book.

SJ410 & SANTANA

A lot of people have cut their teeth off-road in the small-engined SJ, and not without reason. If you wish to have a bit of cheap fun in the rough then an SJ410 with some decent mud tyres is as good a vehicle as you can get. The trouble starts when you start to want a bit more, as the various swaps of engine, transfer box, etc., that are bread and butter to SJ413 owners are denied you, simply because most of them either don't fit or, because of the lack of power, are irrelevant. Also bear in mind that a great deal of the modified kit, even in the UK, comes from the US, and nearly all of that is based on the SJ413/Samurai.

Having said that, most of the suspension modifications covered in the General and Samurai sections are equally viable for the SJ410. However, unless you're going to go to great lengths, and not inconsiderable expense, to get more power you are possibly better off settling for a shackle lift and some slightly larger mud tyres.

An SJ410-engined LJ80 from Norway. (Courtesy Vidar Tøge)

There are some very nice SJ410s around but they're far more difficult to modify than their 1.3-litre counterparts.

SAMURAI & SJ413

The 1.3-litre engined versions of the SJ are the most versatile for modifying. There are a plethora of modifications available, ranging from

The SJ413 is a good base vehicle for off-road modification on a budget.

Body lifts don't alter the suspension but do give greater clearance for larger tyres.

It's possible to produce a very effective homemade body lift.

Front and rear spacers are made of simple drilled round billet aluminium.

the cheap and easy, to the expensive and difficult, with everything in between. In Chapter 2 we discussed the reasons for choosing each of the modifications, in this chapter we'll put them into practice.

Firstly, it should be realised that there are certain differences between the original SJ413 and the later Samurai. The SJ is certainly a capable machine and nearly all the modifications discussed here are equally appropriate to either vehicle, although it should be noted that there may be certain subtle differences in the parts required and you must be careful that the correct kit is obtained.

The major differences are in the length of axle and the spring hanger position. Close inspection of the spring-mountings on the two vehicles will reveal that off-set brackets have been fixed to the chassis rails placing the springs

further apart on the Samurai. This, combined with longer axles, gives a much steadier stance and necessitated the fitting of those telltale wheelarch extensions. Thankfully, this is all just as useful off-road as on, as the wider stance makes the Samurai far less likely to roll over when driven on slopes, and the longer axles make for better articulation. So much for the base vehicles, let's move on to the modifications.

BODY LIFT
Body lift kits are an economical, albeit not hugely technical, way of getting bigger tyres beneath your arches. Whilst lifting the body above the chassis and suspension does give some extra room, the wheelarches don't get any wider, and for that, if no other reason, it's not worth going much above 3in of lift.

The underbody spacers are two-piece affairs.

is threaded. This causes a bit of a dilemma if, for simplicity's sake, you fit a length of 3in box section to give the required lift you are left with a 1in length of unthreaded bolt protruding through the box section, which will have to be threaded with a die or packed out in some way, neither of which are particularly satisfactory and are quite unsightly.

The way round this is to make a composite spacer, the top half (i.e. 1½in) consisting of 2in diameter drilled aluminium, and the bottom half of 4mm walled 60 x 40mm box section laid horizontally. This gives a

Although there is a multitude of body lift kits available, there are basically only two types: the billet spacer and internal nut design, or the two-piece box section and spacer. There's not much to choose between these, although experience has shown that on some makes the internal nut can corrode and become seized within the billet spacer.

The box section and spacer design is easily made and is probably the simplest of the major modifications that can be produced in the home workshop. In basic terms the body is held to the chassis by bolts screwed into captive nuts on the 4 front and rear mounts; and captive bolts welded to strengthened plates in the floor, which hang down through chassis mount plates, on the 6 under-body mounts.

The front and rear mounts require nothing more than a 3in (75mm) long section of round aluminium with a 10.5mm hole drilled centrally, and a 4½in M10 metric fine (1.25) threaded bolt with a new spring washer and the original large flat washer. Few engineering suppliers in the UK carry anything in

With a trolley jack it's best to lift one side of the vehicle at a time.

M10 metric fine, not even threaded stud, so be sure to source some before proceeding. The aluminium needs to be 2in diameter, as this is the maximum size that will fit without fouling the rear bodywork.

The under-body mounts consist of a captive bolt, approximately 2¼in long, of which only the last inch

total of 3in of lift. It also means that the body doesn't have to be raised so high during installation.

The first thing to do is to lift the body from the chassis to enable the spacers to be fitted. There are several ways of achieving this, but it's preferable to lift one side at a time, unless, of course, you have the facilities to lift the entire body in one go.

Because lifting the body without damaging it can be difficult, I recommend cutting a section of timber to the correct length to fit between the body mounts behind the sill. This, atop an ordinary hobby type trolley jack, is sufficient to lift the body clear, whilst being soft enough and has a big enough footprint to cushion the floor panels.

Before lifting there are several bits and pieces that need to be removed or loosened. The body mount nuts and bolts obviously have to come off. Not so immediately obvious, however, are the steering column to steering box clamp; the brake pipe union adjacent to the gearbox on the inside of the offside chassis rail; the petrol tank filler pipe; and the rear fog lamp bracket, where it bolts to the chassis and bumper.

Undoing the brake pipe union is very important, or the rubber hose from the master cylinder will be put under immense strain when jacking the body, and will stop the body lifting sufficiently or pull out of a connector or split. It's also a good idea to disconnect the rear light clusters, which are housed in the bumper and are, therefore, attached to the chassis, and the clips holding the petrol tank sender unit cable. At the front the sidelight/indicators also need to be disconnected.

The 1½in (38mm) aluminium spacer is slid up the captive bolt until it contacts the floor. The box section is then placed on the end of the bolt and the spring washer and nut are fitted inside the box section; loosely, if there is to be any chance of aligning the rest of the parts.

A 60 x 10mm high tensile bolt is then placed through the original

The chassis-mounted brake pipe union needs to be removed prior to attempting to lift the body.

large flat washer, up through the original rubber chassis mount and into the bottom hole of the box section. A spring washer and nut are fitted inside the box section and, once all the spacers are in place, tightened.

The rubber fuel filler pipe will need to be lengthened. This can be cut in half in the upright section and

a 5in length of galvanised tubing fitted in between and held with a couple of jubilee clips.

This just leaves the lights to be reconnected and an extension plate made to fit the brake union to where it bolts to the chassis, a length of 1 x ⅜in flat steel, drilled to take the 4 bolts, will suffice.

So the body lift comprises:
4 no. 3 x 2in - round aluminium
6 no. 1½ x 2in - round aluminium
6 no. 45 x 60 x 40mm - 4mm walled steel box section
4 no. 4½in M10 (1.25) metric fine bolts

Apologies for the mix of imperial and metric units, in my defence all the lift kits are in imperial units although all the component dimensions are in metric. All in all a neat and inexpensive modification. Of course, if you wish you can purchase a ready made kit. Calmini,

The kit from Calmini provides everything required, including bumper lifting irons and a petrol filler pipe extension. (Courtesy Calmini)

for example, manufactures a very good and relatively inexpensive one, which also includes bumper extension brackets to lift the bumpers and fill the gaps left by the body lift.

DRIVETRAIN AND GEARING
Axles

Axle casings are usually pretty good on the SJ series. The Samurai, being slightly longer, gets a bit more stress than it's counterparts, but generally they are quite good enough. If you seem to get through more than your fair share of axle casings, then bracing gussets can be welded in the triangle formed by the underside of the diff housing and the axle tube itself.

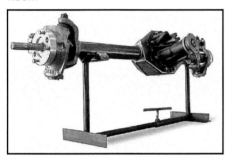

The Spidertrax Sidewinder front axle will cure all your axle and Birfield (Americanism for steering knuckle or CV joint) problems. (Courtesy Spidertrax)

If this is still not good enough, how about a Spidertrax Sidewinder axle? Apart from the immense strength and additional ground clearance, these use Open Knuckle joints for the front steering joints, meaning the end of those hideous grease-filled knuckle covers and associated Birfields that readily give up. Everything is included in the octagonal casing, including the heavy duty 4340 Chromoly 26 spline half shafts, the knuckles and all

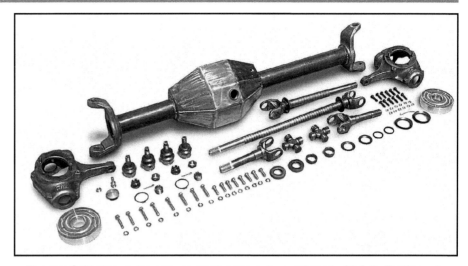

The rear Spidertrax axles can use stock parts or be purchased with fully-floating axle components. (Courtesy Spidertrax)

the required seals and fittings. The axle comes in stock, + 3in and +6in should you require the extra length.

At the rear you have a choice of a Sidewinder Hybrid axle, which is basically a replacement casing that takes the stock Samurai parts, or the Sidewinder Fully Floating rear axle, which mounts the wheel hub on the casing, rather than being a part of the half shaft, which means, not only is the half shaft much stronger than

stock, but you can remove it through the hub without removing the wheel. The specification is similar to that of the front axle, and also uses Samurai front end components to give stock disc brakes on the rear.

Ring and pinion conversion sets

If the Baby Lobster transfer box doesn't give you the gearing you require, then combining it with a

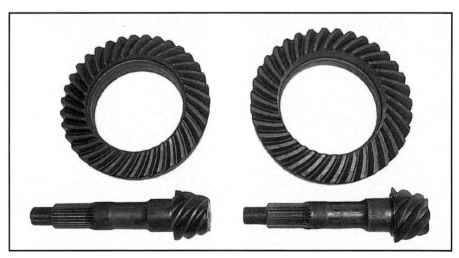

Ring and pinion replacement gears can give gear reductions of up to 50 per cent. (Courtesy Calmini)

new set of ring and pinion gears for the diffs may well be the answer. Sets giving a gear reduction of over 50 per cent should be sufficient for most occasions. Fitting is reasonably straightforward, follow the instructions for fitting a diff locker but simply replace the ring and pinion gears instead.

Rockcrawler gear sets

For the mud usually encountered in the UK it is unlikely, unless you have some seriously huge tyres, that you will require a Rockcrawler gear set. If, however, you are lucky enough to have some mountains on your doorstep, then Calmini does various kits to change the entire internals and dramatically lower the gear ratios to enable you to traverse rocky terrain with ease. Kits are available that give gear ratios from 4.163:1 to as low as 6.5:1 (giving a gear reduction of an enormous 187 per cent). Combine that with the replacement ring and pinions and you should be able to go just about anywhere. The kit contains everything required to rebuild the transfer box, from all the gears, bearings and input shaft, to the gaskets and a detailed instruction book.

Transfer box swap

For a very easy gear lowering conversion on an SJ413/Samurai you can simply swap the transfer box for one out of an SJ410, which will neatly bring your overall gearing back to almost standard with 31in tyres fitted. To give it it's Americanisation it's called a 'Baby Lobster'.

Why a Baby Lobster? Well the full blown Rock Lobster involves quite a bit of machining and welding

Rockcrawler transfer box replacement gear sets can give huge gear reductions. (Courtesy Calmini)

Splitting a transfer box may appear daunting, but with a little care it's relatively straightforward. (Courtesy Calmini)

to combine gears from both the 413 and 410 to give you lower on-road gears to compensate for the bigger tyres, but a much bigger gear reduction for off-road gearing.

This is extremely useful, especially in mountainous areas where low down gearing is necessary to tip toe over boulders and pick your way through rocky passes, such as

Swapping a SJ410 transfer box for the SJ413 unit is easy and reduces the gearing to stock with 31in tyres. (Courtesy Calmini)

Leaving the transfer case brackets attached gives you additional grip and leverage when replacing the unit. (Courtesy Calmini)

those found in the deserts of North America, which is where the Rock Crawler gear conversions originated. Now, of course, you can buy factory produced gear sets that give incredibly low gearing for this type of driving.

In the UK we seem to spend our weekends up to our backsides in mud! So ultra low gearing is not that crucial here. A Baby Lobster will give you a 31in shod truck that drives like it did on standard tyres, and the conversion is quick and easy to do.

The transfer box swap almost reduces gearing to the original overall ratios. The bigger tyres raise the ratio by almost 15 per cent, whilst fitting the Baby Lobster lowers them again by 12 per cent on high ratio and 11 per cent low ratio. The difference is noticeable but it's certainly far more driveable, and at most only 3-4 per cent higher than original. That isn't much more than the difference between a set of worn tyres and a new set.

First off, you'll need a 410 transfer box. There are several different types out there but, thankfully, by far the most common one will fit straight in.

Caution! – Avoid the very early models, as the flanges are much smaller than those on the 413. Not only that, but although two of the shafts are the same size, and therefore the flanges are interchangeable, one of them is not. The easiest way to avoid disappointment is simply to measure the pitch of the boltholes in the flange, and ensure they match up with a potential replacement before parting with your cash; it will then simply bolt in.

Jack the vehicle, front and back, and support on axle stands, the higher the better as access can be a problem, especially if the brackets are left in situ whilst fitting. Drain the oil, remove the speedo cable and tie it out of harm's way. Then, unbolt all of the prop shafts attached to the transfer box, remembering to mark flange positions of shafts on the remaining elements, such as the gearbox, etc., for later re-fitting. If you're removing the forward half of the prop shaft from its slider, this will definitely need to be marked to ensure balance on refitting. If you have an SJ413 with the prop drum handbrake this will have to be removed to allow the handbrake cable to be released. If you're fitting to a Samurai then the entire handbrake mechanism, including back plate, will need to be removed as the handbrake works on the rear hub brakes.

The transfer box is moderately heavy and should be supported securely from below, either with a proper support or a trolley jack with cradle attachment. It's possible to remove the transfer box with the mount bracket in place. Remove the bolts attaching it to the chassis, then undo the other mount bolts and the transfer box can be lowered safely to the ground.

Refitting the transfer box is simply the reverse of the removal procedure, and the whole operation should take less than 2 hours, start to finish.

ENGINE
Engine transplants
Various engines have been dropped into the 1.3-litre models over the years. A popular conversion was the Peugeot diesel engine, but by far the most common engine swap is the Vitara 1.6-litre, 8-valve carburettor engine. Virtually any in-line engine and gearbox combination can be made to fit but, due to the engineering

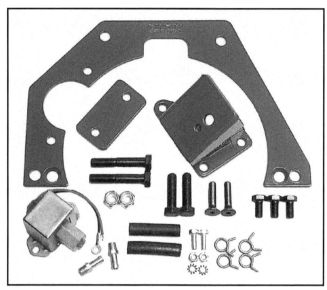

Installation of the 1.6-litre Vitara engine into a 1.3-litre-engined vehicle is straightforward with a conversion kit.
(Courtesy Calmini)

required, we'll concentrate here on the Vitara engine swap, which is relatively cheap, easy to undertake, and provides a significant increase in power and torque. It would be misleading to suggest that this is a straight swap, as neither the gearbox, engine mounts, sump, nor starter motor align properly. Fortunately, however, there are several kits available containing an adaptor plate that connects the engine and gearbox and sorts out the starter motor alignment, and modified engine mounts to align the engine correctly with the gearbox.

Exhaust manifold (header) & system

Probably the best engine modification to make is fitting a free-flow exhaust. A well designed tubular manifold fitted to a corresponding system is a sure fire way of releasing those pent up horses from the 1.3-litre unit. Various companies do aftermarket exhaust systems, probably the best known in the UK is Janspeed in Salisbury. In the US all the usual suspects have an exhaust system; Calmini's Ceramic Coated Header looks particularly nice. Power gains in the order of 18 per cent are usually claimed.

Manual choke conversion

A common area for complaint on all the carburettored models is the auto-choke; fine when it works, but a nightmare to get right when it doesn't. I've changed many of these units over the years, yet still run one on a 15 year old Samurai that starts first time and runs beautifully.

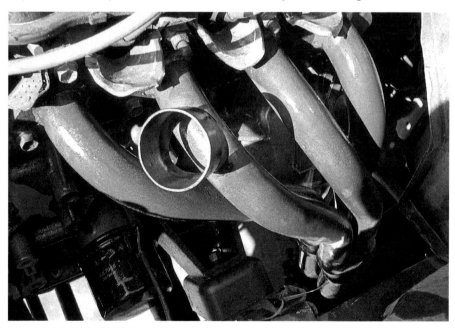

A free-flow exhaust manifold will give a significant boost to the relatively low-powered engines.

Automatic chokes are fine when they work, but can be a nightmare when they go wrong.

If you wish to retain the auto-choke there are two main areas to inspect for defects: the plethora of rubber vacuum pipes; and the carburettor, for spindle wear, cracks or gasket failures, as virtually any air leaks will destroy the carb's performance, and usually the first

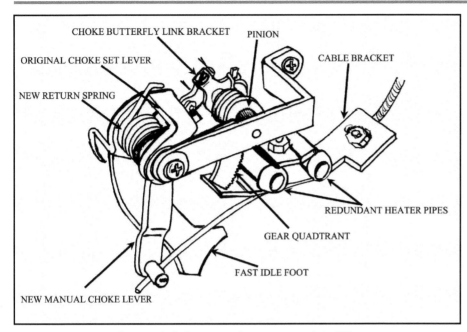

CHOKE BUTTERFLY LINK BRACKET PINION

ORIGINAL CHOKE SET LEVER

CABLE BRACKET

NEW RETURN SPRING

REDUNDANT HEATER PIPES

GEAR QUADTRANT

FAST IDLE FOOT

NEW MANUAL CHOKE LEVER

A manual choke conversion can cure a lot of ills.

The choke conversion kit is easy to fit but final adjustment can be fiddly.

Fortunately, there are various manual conversion kits on the market and fitting is a reasonably simple affair.

The kit contains a set of gears, with a control cable, that simulates the mechanism of the automatic choke. The kit is relatively easy to fit, although fine tuning the mechanism can be time consuming if the engine is to run smoothly.

As the hot water inlet and outlet pipes on the carb body are used to mount the new choke cable securing bracket, the hoses have to be removed and connected together using a section of metal tubing supplied in the kit. **Caution!** – Undertaking this operation on a nice warm engine, with a pressurised cooling system, may result in scalding of any exposed flesh, so wait for the engine to cool down first.

It isn't necessary to remove the carb to fit the kit, as access is gained by simply removing the air intake casing. Removing the distributor cap, with the leads in situ, and placing it across the top of the engine allows greater access to the area with minimum disruption.

The only difficulty is setting the phasing, which is the fast idle roller and the choke flap engagement timing, which should happen as the flap is nearly closed. Adjust the fast idle screw whilst the engine is running cold, and then the idle screw when operating temperature has been achieved. Those annoying starting problems will now be a thing of the past.

SU carburettor conversion

Many people swear by the SU carb as the ideal conversion for the Suzuki engines. The carb is certainly simple to maintain and re-jet, though

thing to show signs of a problem is the auto-choke.

Although this sounds simple enough, you can spend many a happy hour cleaning, checking and reassembling carbs with new gaskets and pipes, only for the same problem to manifest itself.

a totally new inlet manifold casting will be required which can make it a daunting prospect financially.

Weber carburettor conversion

The Weber 32/34 and 32/36 are both commonly used replacements, though they both require adaptor plates to fit the manifold and the air box, and the secondary choke overlaps the manifold casting on the 32/36, which is not ideal. Whichever carb you opt for ensure you have it jetted and adjusted by an expert, preferably on a rolling road. Running a poorly jetted and adjusted carb can rob you of 20 per cent of the engine's potential power, and over-fuel the engine to the extent

The Weber 32/36 carburettor is a common replacement for the stock item.

that number four piston burns out. Why number four? Well, as the engine is inclined slightly backwards that's where all the excess fuel goes.

A problem with Weber downdraughts is that the engine can stall when the vehicle is climbing steeply. This is due to the design of the fuel supply system, which the designers never envisaged would be climbing 1 in 2 cliffs. Some people

Bump stop extensions limit the axle's upward travel, preventing damage to body, tyres and dampers.

reverse the carb to combat this problem, which basically means the carb is running inefficiently and it stalls going downhill instead; not an ideal solution. It's possible to modify the float level, but this can lead to other problems. Generally speaking, these conversions run perfectly well and the pros far outweigh the cons. It is possible to block the fuel bowl vent where it exits through the throttle throat as long as you remember to drill a new vent hole in the casting.

SUSPENSION
Bump stop extensions

Modifying the suspension and fitting longer dampers can mean that under serious articulation the tyres come in contact with the body, or the dampers can 'top out' (i.e. become fully closed) under force. This not only runs the risk of damaging the damper internals, but also of bending the shaft. The problem can be avoided by fitting a piece of drilled box section between the chassis rail and original bump stop, thus limiting the axle's upward travel to a point lower than that where the full stroke of the damper is achieved. A far better solution is to fit raised shock towers to facilitate the fitment of shocks with enough travel. Many companies provide bump stop extensions in their suspension kits.

Flexing shackles

The principle of dislocating shackles

Dislocating shackles allow huge amounts of axle articulation.

Angling the rear dampers inward with an adaptor bar lets you fit longer dampers, giving superior axle travel.

Note that if the shackles have been designed to fit with new poly bushes they can be a bit wide if you're using originals. With the spring end tightened you can use the jack to adjust the height of the chassis eye to fit the shackle. The shackle itself opens, so as long as the eye is above the hole in the shackle you can just open the shackle to fit.

With the shackle fitted turn to the dampers. The fronts are just a straight swap, but to gain greater damper movement the rears can have a new mount bar fitted, which angles the dampers in towards the centre of the vehicle at the top. With the rear dampers removed the mount bar simply bolts straight onto the existing top mounts.

Under extreme articulation the shackles cannot flex enough to allow them to extend to their fullest amount. Some manufacturers offer a combined twister joint within the shackle to combat this and it works extremely well, although the cost is considerably greater than the simple extending version.

You will also require a set of longer brake hoses. On some models, with a central rear brake hose, you can get away with just replacing the front hoses, but it's probably best to do all of them.

The other area that will need attention, if larger tyres are to be used, is the bodywork. Because the extending shackles keep your suspension at almost stock height whilst closed there is little extra room for more rubber. You will, therefore, need to decide before fitting this system if you want to make the most of their capability, in which case you will need some drastic alterations to the wheelarches, or fit a combined suspension lift such as an SPOA, or

is quite simple. Basically, as the ground drops from under a wheel the weight of the axle opens the hinge in the shackle and the wheel stays in contact with the ground, thus continuing to gain traction and propel the vehicle forwards. On the road they behave like simple, stock height shackles.

Fitting the kit is as simple as replacing the shackles and shocks. Jack and support the axle and remove the wheels. Jack the chassis at a convenient point to take the load off the spring, undo the top and bottom nuts and slide the shackle out of the rubber bushes. Then simply offer up the new shackles and fit the bottom bolt through the spring eye.

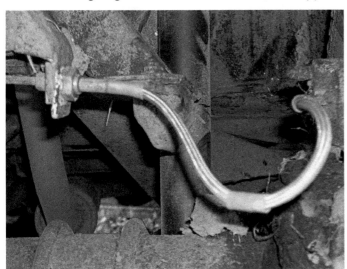

Most suspension modifications will require extended brake lines.

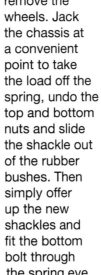

you can, of course, stick to nearly stock tyres.

Extending shackles do affect the on-road manners, though only slightly, but the off-road performance more than outweighs any detractions. I would say there is no other kit that gives you the same amount of manoeuvrability for the price. They will out perform most other types of suspension setup, even with stock springs, with the additional benefit of keeping your centre of gravity low. Combined with longer springs, or an SPOA, flexing shackles can transform your truck beyond all expectations.

Front Panhard rod kit

If you have an SPOA, especially if combined with lifted shackles, missing link shackles or the like, fitted to your Samurai, you will have noticed the corresponding 'wallowing' around corners, and the loss of steering control over large obstacles. There is a simple bolt on kit that will stop all this, the Spidertrax Front Panhard Rod, which provides lateral stability for your Samurai's front axle. This eliminates the common detrimental handling effects on-road of spring over axle conversions and also improves off-road performance. In addition to providing lateral stability, it has integrated bump stop mounts in the U-bolt plates so that front bump stops can be used to control axle articulation. The kit works with both 2in and 2.5in wide springs, though it only works with the offset suspension found on the Samurai, and an SPOA must be fitted.

Hi-steer conversion

If you're running an SPOA you may well encounter bump steer, which is the usual manifestation of not having parallel steering rods. The usual way of countering this is to fit a drop pitman arm or a Z-bar. However, Calmini has come up with a kit for the Samurai that replaces all the steering rods and includes a pair of hi-steer drag links that effectively raises the rods to keep them parallel and also

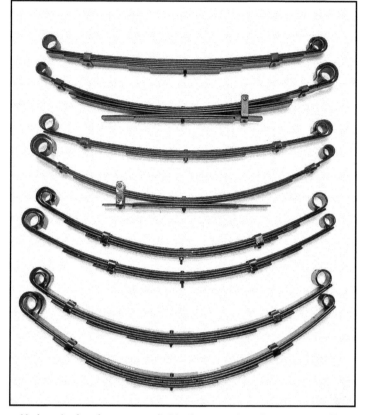
Various leaf springs are available, from stock replacements to 3in lifting items. (Courtesy Calmini)

clear of the springs on an SPOA conversion.

Longer springs

There are various kits on the market with longer springs that give various amounts of lift. If your springs are in need of replacement, fitting lifting springs may well be an option you wish to consider, as they are only slightly more expensive than stock height springs. Calmini supplies springs in various heights from stock to 3in lift.

It's possible to do a homemade conversion along these lines, using the longer rear springs on the front, or even Jeep Wrangler springs. However, it's probably far quicker, easier, and even cheaper in the

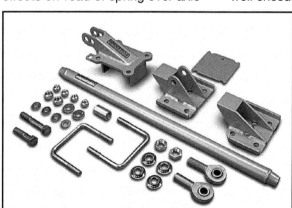
The Spidertrax Panhard rod kit will stop the customary lateral axle travel with an SPOA fitted. (Courtesy Spidertrax)

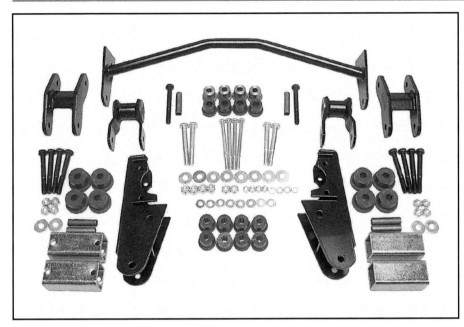

The bolt-on shackle reversal kit gives far superior articulation and ride. (Courtesy Calmini)

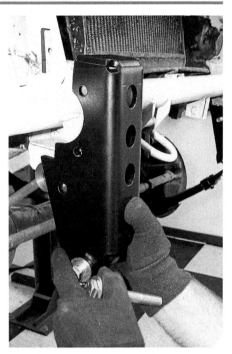

The kit is based on a pair of towers that replace the front shackles with a fixed spring mount. (Courtesy Calmini)

long run, to purchase and fit a new, specifically-designed and balanced kit.

Shackle reversal

It is claimed that fitting a shackle reversal kit increases the articulation on the Samurai, from 11in (279mm) to 18in (457mm) with stock springs! No mean feat. However, with the addition of a complimentary 3in spring lift this is raised to 25in (635mm)! This is serious articulation for a relatively inexpensive bolt on kit. If necessary, you can fit the springs at a later date as your budget dictates.

If you purchase the basic system you will require longer dampers, which are not normally included in the kit. It has been said in the past that you won't need to replace the original dampers. Whilst it is possible to fit the kit with the original dampers, not only would the lack of travel totally negate fitting the kit in the first place, it is also inherently dangerous. If in the future you are likely to fit lifted springs you will have to replace the shocks again, which may be worth considering before purchasing any kit. While you are at it, it's probably a good idea to fit longer brake lines with this kit. If you are going to fit longer springs then it will be a

necessity, but if fitting the springs at a later date it can be left until then.

Basically the kit comprises: two front towers that fit onto the chassis shackle mounts and are braced at the top through the holes in the end of the chassis rails; a brace that goes between these towers to stabilise them; a set of reduced shackles to fit the rear of the front springs; and a set of longer, boomerang shackles for the rear, to keep things even.

So what does all this kit do? Well the theory is that moving the shackles to the rear of the springs on the front suspension will mean that the vector forces involved in mounting an obstacle will be in the same direction as the direction of travel, thus allowing the wheel to rise and fall gracefully, as opposed to the back-jarring crunch experienced with the shackles at the front.

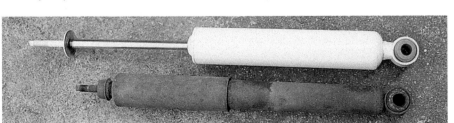

Longer shocks will also be needed to get the most from the kit.

The new front shackles have to be staggered to fit the existing chassis mounts. (Courtesy Calmini)

Fitting the kit only requires a trolley jack, a couple of axle stands and a few spanners. Fit the two front spring towers first as they are arguably the most difficult part. Also, it's far easier to make adjustments fitting the shackle end of the spring last.

If you have trouble removing the rubbers from the springs you can engage an ad hoc puller. Using a socket large enough to go over the shackle rubber and small enough to fit on the spring, put a set screw through the middle with a large washer, small enough to go through the hole in the spring, and wind the bolt up, pulling the rubber out. Then rebuild using the new poly bushes supplied with the kit. Fitting the rear kit involves replacing the rear shackles and shocks and is simplicity itself.

Impressions on- and off-road are favourable: the on-road ride is much superior to standard; and off-road performance is significantly better. One other item worthy of note is the suggestion of brake dive. This can be a serious problem during high speed braking, but it has not been my experience that this kit induces any such manifestation; in fact, totally the opposite.

You should also be aware prior to ordering that there are two different sizes of kit. If ordering from Calmini, for example,

The rear shackles are straightforward longer shackles, doglegged to overcome the travel limiting ears on the shackle mounts. (Courtesy Calmini)

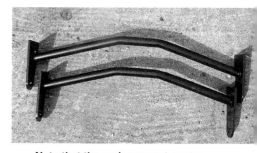

Note that the spring mount centre measurement dictates which kit you require.

the kit sold for the SJ410 also fits the SJ413. The only vehicle that the Samurai kit fits is the Samurai. This is due to the wider stance of the Samurai and its wider spring centres, meaning not only is the front brace bar longer, but there are also certain modifications to the spring towers themselves. Make certain you have the correct kit before placing your order.

The shackle reversal is no slouch, in terms of articulation, for such a simple kit.

To enable longer dampers to be fitted shock tower extensions can be used to accommodate the top damper mount. (Courtesy Spidertrax)

Shock towers

If you've fitted some serious kit to allow your suspension to articulate, it can be galling to find your dampers, even the longer ones fitted with the suspension lift kit, limit the axle movement. To combat this you can install extended upper shock towers. Spidertrax, for example, manufactures a good set which basically raises the top damper mounts, allowing considerably longer dampers to be fitted. This can negate the need for bump stop extensions, as longer damper travel is possible, though this may lead to fouling of the bodywork.

Spidertrax quarter elliptical rear suspension

This setup is probably worthy of inclusion in the Specials Chapter, but as it is now a mainstream modification I will include it here. Imagine half a leaf spring with lots of assistor springs, turned upside down and bolted to the chassis with your rear axle hanging from the end of it, so that the spring acts like a form of flexible trailing arm. This is, in essence, the quarter elliptical rear suspension. This kit is CAD designed and has had several years of trail testing and is not something you are likely to knock up in the shed at the weekend!

The main components are the two pre-welded chassis side plates, which hold the springs and incorporate the lower and upper link mounts, which ensures the dynamics of the suspension stay consistent on any vehicle. The side plates also have alignment pins so that they self-align to the chassis during the installation. The kit includes all links, tabs, rod ends, mounting plates, shock-mounts, pivoting shackles, bump stops, springs, and nuts and bolts required for installation, as well as detailed instructions to ensure easy fitting. This is a weld-on kit so some welding skill is required. It should go without saying that you would have to fit longer dampers and extended brake hoses. These must be sourced separately, although there is a limiting strap included in the kit; one look at the photographs should tell you why.

Spring over axle

SPOA or spring perch over axle appears on the face of it to be a simple conversion – simply sling the axles beneath the springs and it's job done. Unfortunately, the differentials are not centrally-placed in the axles, and cannot, therefore, simply be turned over, and the

The Spidertrax QERS is probably the ultimate bolt-on suspension kit. (Courtesy Spidertrax)

An SPOA can totally transform your vehicle. (Courtesy Calmini)

have built yourself a death trap. And then, of course, there's the shock-mounts to reposition as well, and making some correct length bump stop extensions. So SPOA may not be the simple panacea it first seems.

There have been many kits produced, often including weld on perches that in some way connect with the original perches to ensure correct alignment. However, Calmini now supplies a simple bolt-on kit that is virtually foolproof and gives you that 5in (127mm) of lift that you've been craving.

The kit is basically a set of large cups and plates that clamp completely round the axle, utilising the original perches and bolt holes to exactly position the new perch. With their built in spring-mounts and bump stops, this really is a

Calmini now supplies a simple bolt-on kit that takes away all the guesswork associated with an SPOA conversion. (Courtesy Calmini)

The kit is a simple concept that makes fitting virtually foolproof. (Courtesy Calmini)

spring-mounts that are welded to the bottom of the axle tube need to be removed and re-welded on the top of the axle. This sounds fairly

straightforward but, unfortunately, as many homemade SPOA conversions have shown in the past, get the angles even slightly out and you

driveway bolt-on kit, which is almost impossible to get wrong and is set up to maintain optimum steering angles.

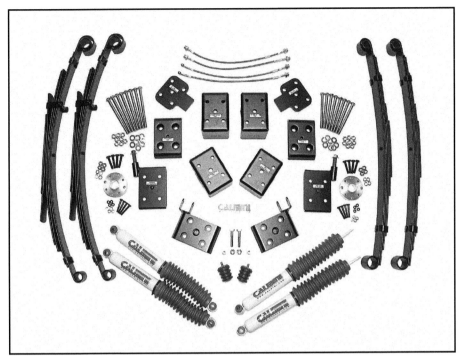

The SPOA/lifting spring combination kit should give you all the suspension modification you'll ever need. (Courtesy Calmini)

Spring relocation pads fit between the spring and axle perch, allowing the axle to be moved forward or backward. (Courtesy Spidertrax)

Spring relocation pads

If you have seriously lifted the suspension and fitted tyres in the order of 31in and above, you may well encounter the tyres fouling on the body, especially at the front, when the steering is at about half lock. The front bumpers and irons are usually removed during modification as, not only are they flimsy affairs prone to damage and corrosion, but they also hinder the vehicle's approach angle. This means there is sufficient tyre clearance to the front to be able to move the axle forwards on the spring to gain clearance at the rear of the tyre.

To do this you can obtain a thin billet aluminium pad that fits between the spring and the perch on the axle, with an offset peg and hole that fit the corresponding peg and hole on the perch and spring. The Spidertrax item has a hole either side of the peg, one offset at ¾in and the other at 1in to enable either offset to be achieved using the same kit.

Chapter 6
Coil sprung vehicles

VITARA, X-90 AND GV
In some quarters of the UK the Vitara has long been regarded as something of a 'hairdresser's car', and dismissed as being irrelevant as far as off-road driving goes. For those in the know, however, it is a serious base for modifying into an off-road giant killer, with additional improvements, not least in ride comfort, over its leaf-sprung siblings.

With the development of the GV and later models there is little doubt the line will carry on well into the 21st century. There is not much to choose between the old style Vitara, the X90, and the early GVs as far as modification goes, so I have lumped them all pretty much together, any particular differences are highlighted through the text. **Note!** – It may sound like a strange thing to say but, if you're buying an X-90 ensure it is a four-wheel drive as there are plenty of two-wheel drive variants out there.

Body lift
Body lifts are just as relevant to coil sprung vehicles as leaf sprung and are covered in the Basic and Leaf Sprung sections. Although the principle is the same the actual kit is not identical for all models, so ensure you have the correct kit before ordering. If manufacturing your own then a simple adaptation of the process in the Leaf Sprung Vehicle section is required.

V6 Suzuki engine swap
If you wish to stay within the Suzuki family for an engine swap there is only one that is reasonably straightforward and worthwhile. This is the 2.0-litre V6 from the

The Vitara is increasingly becoming a base vehicle for serious off-road modification.

The body lift is just as relevant for coil sprung vehicles and the kit is very similar.

The gearbox, dashboard, ECU and steering column all need to be replaced with the V6 engine.

Grand Vitara. As you are changing from a 4- to a 6-cylinder engine the entire wiring loom will have to be changed, which is not a five minute job. The engine swap itself is not exactly a straight exchange either, as the gearbox, dashboard, ECU and steering column also have to be replaced.

There are a number of other small modifications necessary, such as positioning the radiator slightly further forward, although there is room without modifying the existing grille, and modifying the clutch master cylinder mount

and the new steering column to fit. The dashboard will also need to be re-drilled, as the mounts and screw holes are different in the two models. Although all this is a major undertaking it is reasonably straightforward and the results are impressive, the power and torque are far superior to the 1.6-litre four-cylinder engine, and it's a much nicer experience to drive altogether.

Combined with a Calmini 3in suspension lift and 33in tyres, the V6 conversion makes for a very nice truck, though there are some issues with the transmission and the extra

power, and, if the front diff housing is not braced it can eat diff casings at an alarming rate. All in all you may decide it's easier to simply modify a Grand Vitara in the first place, but if you have an ailing 1.6-litre engined Vitara and can source a crash damaged 2.0-litre GV then it's well worth considering as a relatively economical alternative.

It is, of course, possible to fit virtually any engine to anything, and there are more and more V6 and V8 versions around. However, for the purposes of this book, there are no other straightforward swaps.

With a Calmini 3in suspension lift and 33in tyres, the V6 engine conversion makes a very nice truck.

Engine tuning
The other, possibly more reasonable, way of getting extra power is

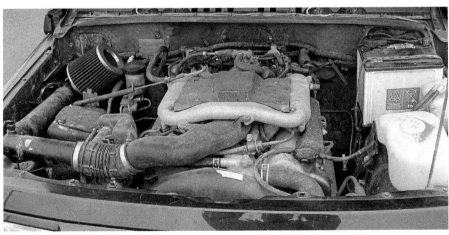

The GV 2.0-litre V6 fits nicely in the old type Vitara engine bay.

A good tubular exhaust manifold can lift power output by up to 15 per cent.

modifying the original engine. A decent tubular exhaust manifold is always a good start, this alone can lift the Vitara's power output by up to 15 per cent and, combined with a Stage I or II head and associated camshaft, and in the case of carburettored models a good carb and inlet manifold, this can easily be raised to 25 per cent. Be careful, though, as bhp isn't everything, top end horses are not worth a hill of beans when crawling over rough terrain, and bhp increases can be to the detriment of low down torque, which is far more beneficial, so check the figures before being separated from any cash.

Live axle conversion

With large amounts of second-hand spares now readily, and cheaply, available it is possible to do a conversion to enable 35in tyres to be fitted without the expense of the complete suspension kit. A set of Pro Comp 1.5in lifting springs is a good starting point, and sets are also readily available now second-hand.

The rear suspension is the easiest area to modify, so concentrate there first. Inspection of the rear suspension mounts reveals a pair of cupped mounts that hold

both the springs and dampers. Carefully cutting these mounts from the chassis and re-welding them 'upside down' gives another 3.5in (88mm) of suspension lift. The coil mount itself will need to be turned at the same time to retain the spring. To locate this amount of lift in the right place the rear radius arms will need to be lengthened, and the rear A-bar, that locates the diff, also needs to be lengthened by five inches. To stop all this from bouncing about, longer than standard dampers will have to be installed.

Up front, the independent front suspension system is notoriously difficult and expensive to modify effectively, but fitting a Samurai live front axle is a relatively cheap and easy solution. It's possible to convert the axle to coil springs as well, but a leaf spring conversion is far easier. You can simply cut the entire front suspension from a Samurai, including the spring hangers, and, with a little chassis modification, simply weld it in place. However, a better ride can be obtained by fitting Santana parabolic front leaves reinforced with Japanese SJ413 assister springs and SJ413 hangers. It may be noted that it's unnecessary to go spring over axle, as the mere installation of the hangers is sufficient to give the same lift as the rear modification.

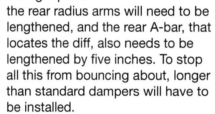

A live front axle conversion is one way to get bigger tyres on a Vitara.

The cupped rear suspension mounts can be cut off and re-welded upside down to give 3.5in of suspension lift.

The front conversion requires leaf spring hangers to be welded to the Vitara chassis rails.

A body lift is required if those 35in tyres are not to come into contact with the body.

The live axle conversion is a good budget modification using available second-hand Suzuki parts.

The original Vitara front differential will need to be installed into the Samurai axle to unify the gear ratios. With this amount of lift the original prop shafts will also need to be binned in favour of custom-built replacements. To get the correct gearing for large wheel and tyre combinations whilst retaining the standard Vitara 16-valve engine, the Vitara's combined gearbox/transfer box has to go, being replaced with standard SJ413 transfer and gearboxes. As the Vitara and Samurai axles are different lengths, a pair of wheel spacers has

Lifting the body leaves the petrol tank behind with the chassis.

to be fitted to align the front and rear wheels.

The body needs some modifications, too. Firstly, a body lift can be fitted, to ensure there is no contact between tyre and wheelarch. This, combined with a set of wheelarch extensions, such as those fitted to wide-wheeled, lowered, street versions, not only ensures the vehicle keeps on the right side of the law but can also come in very useful when the mud begins to fly, if only for the spectators!

It should be noted that if a body lift is fitted, front and rear bumper brackets will need to be modified or new custom bumpers fitted, to fill the gap between body and bumper, as the bumpers are fitted to the chassis.

All in all this is a good modification, if a little unorthodox, especially for those with plenty of time and skill but a limited budget. It gives superb ground clearance, especially when fitted with 35 x 12.50 x 15 tyres, which it easily accommodates, and has the additional benefit off-road of a live front axle.

Tank lift

If you have a body lifted Vitara it will soon become apparent that a major limiting factor to its off-road capability is the departure angle; notably restricted by the petrol tank. A tank guard is installed as standard on the Vitara, but in severe conditions it won't last very long. The vulnerability of the tank is accentuated by the body lift as the tank is attached to the chassis rails. So, when the body is lifted the tank is left behind.

Run the tank dry; a full petrol tank weighs a considerable amount and is difficult to remove safely. Place a trolley jack under the centre of the tank, with a foot square piece of ½in ply on the business end so as not to buckle the guard or the tank. The Vitara has a pressurised fuel

It's easy to modify the tank mounts to raise the tank in line with the body lift.

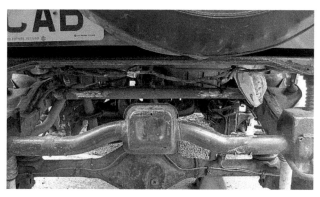

The chassis tank mounts removed.

The front tank mounts have to be bolted direct to the chassis cross rail.

system so take off the petrol cap and release the pressure. Remove the fuel pipes, access is not a problem with a body lift installed, but be prepared for fuel to drain back from the pipes. Remove the four bolts holding the tank and guard to the chassis. Now gently release the jack whilst supporting the tank to ensure it does not fall whilst it is being lowered.

With the tank removed you can see what needs to be done to lift the tank. The rear mounts can simply be cut off the chassis rail and the stubs ground flat. These are then re-welded onto the inside of the top of the same chassis rail. Before cutting, measure the required amount, i.e. the height of the body lift. Then remove the whole front bracket because it is impossible to get the tank back in with them on.

The only way to leave enough room to manoeuvre the tank into position is to drill the chassis rail and fit bolts through it. The rail

is not of the strongest material and a compromise has to be made on bolt size or the hole in the tube will be too large and will weaken it too much to support the tank. Use the tank guard as a template over the rear mounts and mark the front rail through the boltholes in the guard legs. Then, ensuring the holes are vertical in both planes, drill the chassis to the required diameter.

Before re-installing the tank, take the opportunity to strip all the breather pipes from the top of the tank, give it a good rub down, and repaint it with a good quality, corrosion-resistant paint. The breather pipes are prone to rust at their connection to the tank, and it's a good idea to give them a close inspection. If the breathers are not to foul the rear floor, two spacers will need to be fitted between the rail and the tank. Fit locking nuts to these bolts so you don't have to over-tighten them and deform the tubing.

To get the tank into position you need to push the rear seam well up over the chassis rail until the front is in, then allow it to fall back once the front is in position. In the correct position if the front of the tank is allowed to fall forward it will stop against the chassis rail and

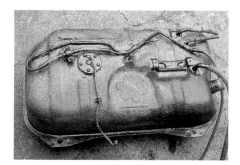

Give the tank and its connecting pipes a thorough examination, clean and paint, as they are prone to corrosion.

With the tank reinstalled the extra clearance is obvious.

The front springs are not as easy to fit as they might be due to the suspension configuration.

stay in place. The guard can now be re-positioned. It cannot be installed straight up as there is insufficient clearance, and it needs to be over the top of the newly installed rear mounts. However, it should be possible to get it in to one side of the mounts. Once the guard has been lifted into place, slide the legs over the chassis mounts. Support the guard in place with a trolley jack and install all the holding bolts. It is then just a case of refitting the supply, return, breather and filler pipes. Full modification should only take a couple of hours.

Uprated coil springs

With major suspension modifications to the Vitara's independent coil sprung suspension being relatively expensive, it may be comforting to know that there is an economic alternative. There are various 1.5in (38mm) raised spring kits on the market nowadays and they are a relatively simple job to fit.

Raised spring kits, combined with a 3in (75mm) body lift and longer dampers, mean that you can get 30in or even 31in tyres under your

A body lift and longer springs will give sufficient clearance for 30in tyres.

Vitara if you're willing to trim a little metal from the wheelarches and bumpers.

The most difficult springs to change are those on the front, where the weight of the engine and gearbox means the springs are fairly strong even in standard form. The easiest, although not the quickest, way to fit the front springs is to drop the wishbones, replace the springs and jack the suspension back into position.

The quickest way is to use a

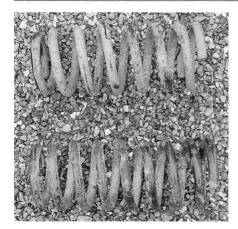

New springs should be similarly rated and longer than standard, not just heavy-duty versions.

Longer springs allow clearance for bigger tyres.

spring compressor to shorten the springs until they are small enough to come out of the suspension, you will need to remove the anti-roll bar to allow the suspension to drop as far as possible. Access is not easy, especially with a spring compressor, as space is limited within the suspension setup.

The springs on the rear are far easier to replace, as they're not of the same strength, don't have the engine and gearbox to support and,

being a live axle, they don't have a wishbone configuration so are easier to access.

Note! – Be careful when choosing new springs; those that are simply thicker, and therefore stronger, do nothing to increase your off-road ability other than lift the vehicle, what you're looking for is longer springs with a similar, or even lower, spring rate, so that they will allow the axles to articulate.

With correctly rated springs ride quality and handling are markedly better, both on- and off-road, ironing out a lot more of those annoying potholes. Body roll should be noticeably reduced, as is the tendency to skip round bumpy corners, especially with new gas shocks.

Off-road, the differences are no less noticeable, the ground clearance and axle articulation are increased, and much of the improved ability off-road that is attributed to the superior ground clearance is down to increased traction from greater articulation.

You should not encounter any change in steering geometry or excessive tyre wear with uprated springs, as the steering geometry has not significantly altered. However, as with any other suspension modification, it's worth having the setup checked at your local garage.

3in suspension lift
This lift kit is synonymous with Calmini, the Suzuki modification specialists from Bakersfield, California. Even in the UK virtually all lifted Vitaras, other than those with simple spring lifts, sport this kit. As discussed in the Principles of Modification it is difficult to overcome certain design restraints when modifying independent suspension. The control arms pretty much limit the amount of travel possible and it is impossible to get around this problem. An extra 1.5in in the form of a spring lift is pretty much the limit.

To overcome this, Calmini set about trashing virtually the entire

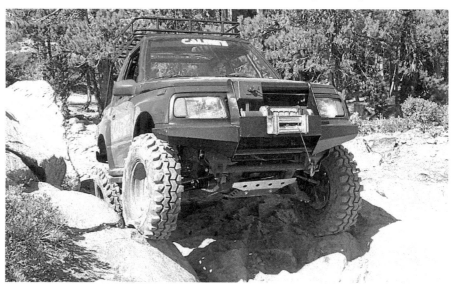

The Calmini suspension lift is synonymous with lifted Vitaras. (Courtesy Calmini)

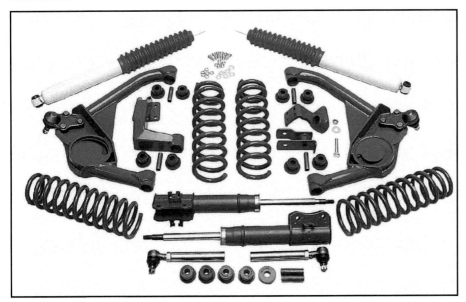

The kit replaces virtually the entire front suspension system. (Courtesy Calmini)

With the suspension and body lift combination, it's possible to fit 35in tyres with a little trimming of the bodywork.

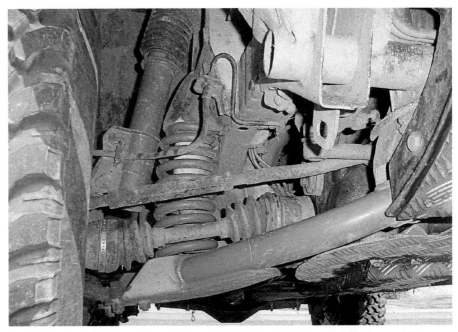

With early teething troubles addressed, the kit is a great modification for any Vitara, X-90 or Grand Vitara.

reach of the home mechanic. This bolt-on conversion alone will allow the fitting of 30in tyres. Combined with a 3in body lift kit you can fit 32in tyres with no fouling. It is possible, however, with a little gentle trimming of the wheelarches, to fit 35in tyres without any problems.

It's fair to say that, initially, people installing this kit had some issues with the aluminium diff housings. With the increase in stress to the front diff mount, many diff housings were wrecked by the bracket ripping out of the diff casing under extreme load. This has been pretty much eradicated now with the development of a steel bracing

suspension system, replacing it with new, modified, parts. The control arms are replaced with longer tubular steel items, which can handle much greater articulation, and the additional ride height is supplied by 3in over standard springs. Calmini also utilises new upper V-links with adjustable high misalignment Heim joints (spherical rod ends) which allows the pinion angle to be adjusted. Combined with the front

axle drop brackets, this gives a huge increase in articulation. Longer trailing arms, springs and dampers allow the rear to keep up with the front.

Fitting the kit is well within the

collar that positively positions the diff casing. It is possible to replace the axle with either an aftermarket steel axle or, if you can find one, a steel axle from certain models of Grand Vitara.

Gearing

With all this extra rubber spinning round, the original gearing will be virtually useless, although there are 5.38:1 ring and pinion sets available. Calmini does just such

Rockcrawler transfer gear set conversions are available for the Vitara, but they don't reduce on-road gearing. (Courtesy Calmini)

are likely to want off-road. However, due to the design of the integral transfer box, the on-road gearing will remain standard, and you're likely to notice a serious drop in performance with 35in tyres on stock gearing.

There is, however, another conversion, developed by a UK company, which can overcome this problem. This involves making the internal transfer box redundant, and fitting a Samurai transfer box, complete with Rockcrawler gears, behind the main gearbox. This means you can fit the 6.5:1 Rockcrawler gearing for the Samurai transfer box to the Vitara, which not only lowers the low range by 187 per cent but also reduces the high range box by 20 per cent. Combined with the low ratio ring and pinions, this should be low enough for any eventuality. Don't be tempted unless you're going to be running huge tyres or you want go at caterpillar crawling speed.

Fitting the Samurai transfer box is not a simple bolt-on affair by any means, but should be within the reach of a competent machine shop. The original Vitara transfer box abuts the gearbox and appears as one unit. It is possible, however, to remove the transfer box from the gearbox, but this is where the expertise comes in. It's then necessary to blank off the rear

The rear of the gearbox needs to be blanked off with a casting that incorporates a new rear bearing. (Courtesy Dave Jones)

a set, for example, and these are okay for increases up to 29-30in tyres. For tyre sizes above that, the Rockcrawler gear conversion sets give a 4.24:1 ratio which equates to a 134 per cent reduction. This should be fine up to the biggest tyres you

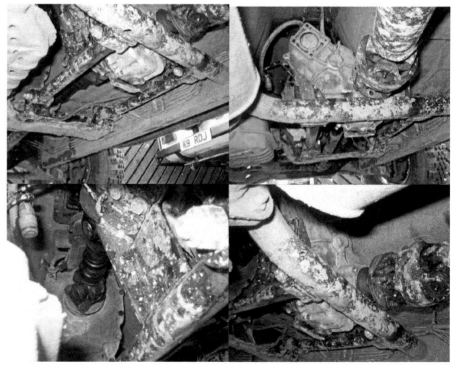

A simple bolt-on conversion will soon be available. (Courtesy Dave Jones)

of the gearbox with a casting that incorporates a new rear bearing.

New prop shafts will also be required between the rear of the shortened gearbox and the Samurai transfer box, and between the transfer box and the front and rear axles. The transfer box is not just a bolt-in either, which probably comes as no surprise, and custom-made brackets will be needed to hold it all in place on the chassis; these will need to be substantial to resist the torque passing through the transfer box. Whilst modifying the transfer box it is also possible to convert to a 2-wheel drive low gear. Whilst this is not essential, it can be utilised on occasion to get you out of a sticky situation.

The company that undertakes this conversion, RS Mfg of Leominster in Herefordshire, is also in the process of developing a simple bolt-on conversion that means the driveway mechanic will be able to fit a similar conversion in the near future. Most of these conversions are exported to the USA, so it should be possible to obtain one of these kits off the shelf whichever side of the Atlantic you may hail from. The company also manufactures double and triple boxes for the Vitara, and SU manifolds for the SJ and Vitara, to name a few of its range of products.

JIMNY
It would not be too much of an exaggeration to describe the Jimny as the Samurai of the future, as far as the off-road community is concerned. It's relatively cheap, has a similar 1300cc engine and, with its coil sprung live axles and real off-road transmission, it's ripe for modification. They may be beyond

Jimnys are quickly becoming common off-road. (Courtesy KAP Suzuki)

the pocket of most people as an off-road toy at the moment, but they are already becoming a common sight at off-road events.

One company that has done much to increase the profile of the Jimny off-road in the UK is KAP in Keighley, West Yorkshire. It has developed many modified pieces of kit since the Jimny was launched and has built, possibly the ultimate Jimny, the 3.5-litre V6 Cosworth-engined Bandit.

Bumpers
Whilst the overhang on either end of the Jimny is not huge by any

It's possible to include a new tubular bumper in the roll cage design.

means, there is some gain to be had by replacing the stock items with tubular steel units. Not only is there a significant increase in attack and departure angles, but the stock bumpers are not really man enough for serious off-road use in any case.

On at least one conversion the rear bumper has been incorporated into the rear roll-cage design. This has had a drop down rack fitted, holding the spare wheel, jerry can and farm jack.

Lifting springs and spring spacers
More suspension travel and some much needed additional height for bigger tyres are provided by 3in lifting springs. These can be supplemented by 2in spring spacers to give 5in of lift over stock, which is enough to let you run 30in tyres with only a little judicious trimming of the wheelarches.

Fitting is fairly straightforward as there are no lower control arms, as with the Vitara, because of the live axle setup, so it's similar to the rear Vitara spring installation. Longer replacement dampers will be required to handle all that extra axle movement, though, as will longer brake hoses.

With this amount of axle movement keeping the springs in a good arc is difficult. With this in mind, KAP spring

Lifting springs and spacers give a good suspension lift.

Sliding spring dislocaters are a great step forward in the development of Jimny suspension modifications. (Courtesy KAP Suzuki)

turrets are moved 2½in further forward which means the springs sit at the correct angles when the axle drops.

Spring dislocaters

A major problem with coil springs is making the spring elongate enough to give good articulation, yet still retain its normal characteristics. This is usually achieved by allowing the spring to disengage from the chassis at extreme articulation, and employing a relocating cone in the centre of the spring mount that guides the spring back to its original position upon closure.

KAP has redesigned this mount into a sliding plate design. Instead of the spring becoming detached from its seat, the seat itself has the spring bolted to it, and has a tube fitted to the rear that slides in the new chassis mount, allowing an additional 8in of spring drop, giving ample movement for serious articulation.

Transfer box

With larger tyres the gearing needs to be reduced if the maximum advantage is to be had. Fortunately, Suzuki saw no reason to drastically alter the existing transfer box, and similarly to the Samurai, sufficient gear reduction can be achieved by bolting in an SJ410 transfer box. Obviously, as the Jimny has a rear drum handbrake, the transfer handbrake and back plate can be completely removed. This is essential in any case as the Jimny mounting bracket, which must be swapped for the original SJ410 item, fouls the back plate. Other than that the swap is fairly straightforward and similar to that outlined in the Samurai chapter, although new or modified mounting brackets are required. Another fly in the ointment is the speedometer sensor, which is mounted on the transfer box and will need remounting, which is not as simple as it sounds. Another of those simple looking modifications

that turns out to be rather more interesting than it first appears.

Twister radius arms

On the normal Jimny the radius arms are fixed, and not overly strong for the rigours of off-road driving. To combat this, KAP has developed twisting radius arms. The entire radius arm is replaced with a tubular steel affair that ends near the chassis bush. The bush end is manufactured from threaded steel rod, and screws into the end of the tubular arm. This screw allows the end of the radius arm to rotate, thus freeing the axle from any lateral restraint and allowing it to articulate independent of the radius arms. Considerably stronger than the stock items, KAP's arms ensure that the radius arms don't bend when off-road.

To fit these, all you need to do is to undo the bolts that attach to the axle mount and the chassis mount, drop the original arms, and fit the new arms and bushes.

Chapter 7
Off-road driving

For those of you new to off-roading it is likely your vehicle will be far more capable than you are to start with and you'll be surprised what it is capable of, even in standard form. Suzuki 4x4s, with their independent transfer boxes and low ratio gearing, are particularly adept off-road, unlike many of the later supposed off-roaders, enabling them to drive incredibly difficult terrain. To get you started, this chapter will give you a few pointers to driving the common obstacles you are likely to encounter. First, though, a quick rundown on preparing your vehicle for the rigours of off-roading.

VEHICLE PREPARATION
Before taking your pride and joy into the rough, a quick inspection to remove or protect any parts that might get damaged is well worth the effort. Pay particular attention to the area below the doors and at the front

Many 4x4s don't have a low ratio transfer box, which severely limits their off-road ability.

and rear of the vehicle. There are all manner of things here that risk being ripped off.

Off-road centres are littered with driving and fog lights. Any fitted below bumper level should be repositioned, as should any number plates that protrude below bumper level. This may all seem irrelevant, but they are costly and annoying to keep replacing.

Tie up any rear mud flaps, and reposition or remove any trailer light sockets. Because of the way these protrude, they're usually the first things to get smashed off. If not required, remove any low tow hitches. Although highly unlikely it will be damaged, tow hitches can severely hinder your departure angle and could get you stuck high and dry. There is an argument for leaving the tow bar in place to protect the petrol tank, but

Additional lights, mud flaps, etc., should be removed or secured prior to venturing off-road.

Off-road sites are littered with towing light sockets and fog lights that have been ripped off.

Radio aerials are often broken off, so retract them if you can.

it's better by far to fit a new heavy-duty steel tank guard and, if you have a body lift, consider lifting the tank out of harms way.

Other obvious and easy areas to look out for are radio aerials, which should be retracted as much as possible, and door mirrors, which should be folded into the vehicle to prevent them being torn out of the bodywork.

Underneath, the first stop is the engine bay. It's usually recommended that the distributor cap be sealed with silicon grease. Whilst this is a very effective way of sealing these areas, silicon grease can melt in the extreme heat of the engine bay on an off-road day, especially in summer, and leave you defenceless against water ingress. Spray everything in sight liberally with a silicon sealant and, unless totally submerged, it should be okay. The Suzuki 4x4 range is designed to be driven in water and, subsequently, all ignition components are as high and as far back as possible.

Other precautions you may be encouraged to try might include fitting a rubber glove over the distributor. One lead through the tip of each finger, tied underneath. The only time I tried this, the glove filled up with water and it was only the fact that I had sprayed the distributor with sealant first that saved the day. The components in modern 4x4s should be of sufficient tolerance to ensure

Trees and rocks love door mirrors.

that silicon spray is adequate to seal them.

Still under the bonnet, check the battery terminals. They should be clean and tight, as should the securing bracket. Check the main earth, alternator and starter

A simple spray ignition sealer is usually all that's required to waterproof a Suzuki engine.

connections. Check that all cables, particularly handbrake cables, which are the usual culprits, are out of the way and securely fastened. Catch one on a root and your day will come to a sudden end, as will the cable.

Sudden immersion in water can kill your gearbox, transfer box and axles. A lot of more serious off-road

Battery terminals should be clean and tight, and the battery securely fastened.

vehicles have breathers fitted to all these components. If you don't know where they are, find them, and check they are clear and intact. Breathers stop water being drawn in as the casing cools making the internal pressure drop. If you have only poppet valves fitted, you will need to at least check, and probably replace, the oil in all of these areas following any serious immersion, then fit some breather pipes.

Make sure your floor plugs are well fitted, as the pressure of driving into water can have them popping out, with all the associated disruption a vehicle full of water causes. Finally inside, make sure you have a comprehensive tool and recovery kit, and that it is securely boxed up and fastened to the interior of the vehicle, as should be everything else that is liable to leap about whilst driving off-road. **Caution!** – This cannot be stressed enough. Should you be unfortunate enough to have an accident, anything that is unsecured becomes a missile and can cause severe injury or even death.

So called side-rails and steps are worse than useless off-road. They are not substantial enough for sill protection and severely reduce

the vehicle's ground clearance and thus the ramp breakover angle. Remove them before venturing off-road. These are not to be confused with nerf bars which are there to protect your sills and assist progress over large, hard obstacles.

Give all tyres, including the spare, a thorough inspection for splits, cuts, bulges, or items buried in them. A blow-out on an off-road site is at best disgustingly dirty and annoying, at worst, dangerous. A quick check every now and then will lessen the chance of you getting a blow-out.

Reducing tyre pressure can give extra grip due to the increased footprint, but also reduces ground clearance and increases the chances of tyre sidewall damage.

You can also reduce the pressure in the tyres to increase the footprint and, therefore, the traction of the tyres. Reducing the pressure to half its normal road value, and even below 10psi, can be awesome; the difference in traction has to be seen to be believed. However, two things should be considered; first, running tyres at low pressure can have them off their rims; and second, ensure that either the site has a compressor or you have some other method of re-inflating your tyres before you leave the site. You

Don't forget to engage your freewheeling hubs before venturing off-road.

don't want to drive on-road with deflated tyres. Not only will you ruin the tyres, but you'll need arms like a gorilla to steer the vehicle; the handling is atrocious and it's illegal. Finally, don't forget to turn those freewheeling hubs to lock. I have lost count of the number of times I have seen people struggling off-road because they have not engaged their front hubs, myself included.

DRIVING TECHNIQUES
Ruts
Let's start with the most commonly encountered off-road obstacle. Almost everyone who ventures off-road in the UK will encounter ruts. To a certain degree your ability to drive over ruts is determined by one factor alone: ground clearance. Basically, the more rubber you can get under your vehicle the deeper ruts you can drive. As discussed in Chapter 2, this is a compromise between height and centre of gravity. That aside, there are certain techniques that will keep you moving.

Most of the time you will be driving along ruts rather than across them, some of which will have been churned up by vehicles with larger diameter tyres, especially on green lanes used by farm vehicles. In this

Driving along ruts is fine so long as you have sufficient ground clearance.

If muddy ruts have no firm base, aggressive tyres can simply dig you a big hole to sit in.

ways. That innocuous looking puddle can be 18 inches deep and you suddenly find yourself grounded. I was once trundling along a nice dry green lane with grass growing in the middle only to be suddenly brought to a crashing halt as the diff housing was torn in half by a huge lump of rock hidden in the grass. So be warned.

Another major danger with ruts relates to knowing the direction your wheels are pointing. Your vehicle will happily travel along the ruts like a train on a track. Whilst you are in deep ruts this is not necessarily a problem. When you come to a shallower area, however, the tyres may suddenly gain purchase on the side of the rut and the vehicle will unexpectedly lurch sideways out of the ruts. This not only brings the soft contents of the vehicle (i.e. you) in contact with the hard parts of the vehicle shell, but can roll the vehicle. So make sure you know which way your wheels are pointing and keep them straight.

The very fact that there may be more grip on the sides of the rut can be an advantage, however. If you're struggling for grip, turning the steering

instance, you'll definitely be limited by your ground clearance. There is no magic driving technique that will make up for all four wheels being off the ground! Of course, you can drive between the ruts if they are too deep; but where's the fun it that?

Ruts can be deceptive in many

Your vehicle will follow deep ruts whichever direction your wheels are pointing. If the front tyres suddenly grip, however, the results can be spectacular.

from side to side will cause the tyre tread to cut into the sidewalls of the trench on each side and may give you sufficient extra grip to slowly 'walk' your way onto firmer ground.

Crossing ruts is not as easy as it looks, but is relatively straightforward if carried out correctly. Even deep ruts can be traversed if approached at roughly 45 degrees. This way you reduce the chances of becoming cross-axled, as usually only one wheel will be out of contact with the ground at any one time. Also, you should not foul the underside, as at least one wheel will be on high ground thus raising the vehicle clear of the obstruction.

Becoming cross-axled whilst crossing ruts can be avoided by crossing the ruts at an angle.

Deep mud is fun to drive through but not much fun to get stuck in.

Second gear low ratio and steady momentum will see you through most muddy situations.

Mud

The word mud covers a whole host of conditions. It ranges from coloured water, boggy peat and gritty loam to thick adhesive clay, and the necessary driving techniques are almost as varied. The one to avoid is mud over chalk. This is akin to Teflon, only more slippery, especially after it's had a convoy of vehicles over it. If you are last in a column of vehicles watch out. Sitting in a small hole with a few inches of mud in it with all four wheels spinning helplessly may be funny to watch but it's embarrassing when you're the one who's driving.

There's a much used mantra off-road that you should drive 'as fast as necessary and as slowly as possible, this is certainly true when driving in mud. This is one obstacle where a little speed can be your friend. This does not mean thirty miles per hour I hasten to add, but a bit of momentum will help get you through those sticky patches. To get the torque down efficiently you will need second or third low ratio. This will not give the spin inducing wheel speed of first gear and will also not stall at the first sign of resistance.

Gently build up the revs as you approach the obstacle and don't let the power off until you reach terra firma on the other side. If the wheels start to spin, drop the revs, but once you regain traction build the speed up again. This doesn't work in all cases, and sometimes you're better off leaving the wheels spinning so long as you still have forward momentum. This is where experience will tell. Try not to accelerate or brake quickly; smooth actions will usually get you through where spinning wheels will just dig you deeper into the mud.

Deep water

Although you may like driving through water your truck doesn't. Water will get into every nook and cranny and, depending on its mineral content, will destroy starter motors, alternators, brakes, and electric fans, clog radiators, and, if you're really unlucky and manage to breath some into your air intake, take out your engine as well. That's the downside. The upside is the sheer exhilaration of driving through water which is lapping at your windowsills.

Much of the 'knack' of driving deep water is down to vehicle preparation, which is covered elsewhere. Basically, you'll need a raised air intake, and the ignition system will need to be sealed. Even with the best prepared vehicle you still need to know the depth of the water before driving into it. Even at

A well-prepared vehicle can drive through surprisingly deep water.

If attempting to drive in deep water, a
snorkel is essential.

Although inadvisable to stop in deep water, sometimes it's unavoidable ...
(Courtesy Steve Abbot)

Enter the water slowly to prevent water
splashing up over the engine.
(Courtesy Jon Gilbert)

off-road centres you can't be certain
what the depth of water is. Unless
the crossing is specifically marked
you have two choices. Either prod
around with a stick, wading out into
the area you intend to drive through
to check the depth or wait for some
other idiot to drive through it first.

With the depth issue resolved
you can enter the water. Enter slowly
in second gear, low ratio, at about
5mph. Driving into deep water at
breakneck speed may be fun and
look spectacular but you won't look
so clever sitting in the middle of a
lake with a dead engine.

You will notice a bit more power
is required to drive through deep
water, due to pushing a couple of
tons of water out of the way, but
make sure you maintain your speed.
As you drive deeper in you should
see a bow wave forming in front of
the bonnet. This bow wave not only
helps you keep your momentum
going but, just as importantly, forms
a trough behind it which keeps the
water level in the engine bay at a
minimum, thus protecting the engine
ancillaries and ignition.

I should mention that it is
inadvisable to stop whilst in deep
water as that beautiful bow wave
you managed to create on the way in
will then wash up under the engine
bay, drowning your engine. If you
stall the engine, you may also be
unlucky enough to get water surging
up the exhaust pipe, straight through
the open valves and into the engine.
Exhaust pressure is sufficient to
keep the water out of your exhaust,
but stop the engine and you'll have
lost any means of preventing water
ingress.

Hills

You will be pleasantly surprised,
or possibly scared witless, at the
angles your vehicle will climb and,
even more impressively (as you
are looking downhill), descend.
If you don't abuse it, it can be an
exhilarating experience. **Caution!**
– Never try to turn round on a steep
slope. It will almost certainly end in
tears.

The classic approach to driving
downhill is to use low ratio first gear,
don't touch the brakes, and don't
touch the clutch. Well, that's fine if
you have loads of engine braking.
In a Suzuki, however, on a long,

Climbing hills can be exhilarating and your vehicle will go places you wouldn't have thought possible. (Courtesy KAP Suzuki)

Steep hills are great fun but can be dangerous, so be careful.

A bit of momentum can be required to get up a steep hill and is less dangerous than making it almost to the top and having to reverse back down.

and I do mean gently. Stamp on the brakes in panic and you'll get to the bottom quicker, but not necessarily on your wheels.

If there are ruts available so much the better as they can aid stability as you descend, stopping the rear end trying to overtake the front. If not, descend as vertically as possible, keeping a firm grip on the wheel and ensuring the wheels stay aligned with the ruts. **Caution!** – Never, ever, descend with the clutch disengaged. If the vehicle gets out of

shape apply a little throttle to regain control.

Uphill is slightly different as you don't have gravity to assist you. You may well need a bit of speed before you start to climb, and you'll have to feed in more power as you ascend to keep your momentum going. As soon as you clear the hill shut the throttle right off.

If you don't have enough power or traction to get up and you find yourself stuck three-quarters of the way up a steep hill and the only way is down, don't panic. Keep your foot firmly on the brake, apply the handbrake but do not take your foot off the brake. The handbrake only brakes two wheels on some models and even with a prop brake it is nowhere near as efficient as the footbrake. Engage reverse. Release the handbrake, then slowly let your foot off the brake as you lift your foot off the clutch. Keep the steering straight and you should roll slowly down to the bottom of the hill. This is inherently more dangerous than a forward descent as you effectively have rear-wheel steering and all the weight of the engine, etc., is trying to turn your vehicle round, so be careful. If you manage to stall the engine simply follow the above procedure except that you select reverse gear and, with the clutch pedal up and the ignition turned on, release the brakes, the engine will fire as soon as you roll backwards ensuring that the vehicle is under full control immediately.

Side slopes

As a general rule, don't. This is probably the most dangerous situation you will encounter off-road. Even in a well-equipped vehicle, rolling sideways down a steep hill is

steep hill you would probably be doing about 40mph by the time you reached the bottom. One of the areas where that diminutive engine lets you down is engine braking. It doesn't have any, so you have no option but to use the brakes. Gently apply the brakes to check the vehicle's speed, if necessary,

Driving side slopes at an off-road centre will give you a feel for it should you have to do it for real.

Side slopes made of sand are accidents waiting to happen.

downhill side or bumps on the uphill side can be enough to have you over. The ground can give way if it is sand or clay, wet or dry, or if there are any changes in soil condition along the traverse. Under controlled conditions at off-road sites, etc., you can practice side slopes in relative safety to get the feel of your vehicle in that situation. Off-road for real, however, if you can avoid driving a side slope, do so.

However, if you should ever find yourself in the position where you have to traverse a side slope, it's

better that you should know how. Firstly, if you never get out of your truck for any other reason do it for this. Survey the terrain like your life depends on it, because it probably does. Anything on the vehicle that raises the centre of gravity should be removed, such as roof racks full of equipment, for instance. All heavy items should be secured, and all the windows closed. If the worst should happen you don't want to be half way out of a window when your side makes contact with the ground, nor do you want to be hit with a flying bottle jack or similar.

As a rule of thumb, your vehicle will probably be safe up to about 30 degrees. However, raise the suspension, fit larger tyres, or put on a body lift, and forget it. Some modern vehicles have a nice inclinometer atop the dash. If you are approaching the danger point this will come in very handy, but only for

at best scary and at worst fatal and that's not considering the mess it will make of your truck on the way down. There are so many dangers, many of them unpredictable, that it's impossible to say with any certainty if a slope is driveable before you attempt it and that is why it is so dangerous. Any hollows on the

Make a mistake on a side slope and you won't stop until you reach the bottom.

you to bite on in a desperate attempt to stop yourself from falling out of the window.

The usual driving conditions apply, of course, low ratio first, etc. Grip the steering wheel firmly, remembering to keep your thumbs out of the spokes, and drive across the slope. Just let the engine pull you along on tickover, if possible. If you start to slide a little just let it go. Don't try to correct the steering uphill. **Caution!** – Never turn uphill. If you feel the vehicle begin to lift off then turn down hill and accelerate. Better to be at the bottom of the hill in one piece than upside down.

Keep your thumbs out of the steering wheel at all times when driving off-road, or learn by bitter experience.

Grass

Tall grass peppered with big seed heads will quickly block your radiator core and can lead to overheating, especially as, by their very nature, seed heads are most likely to be there when the weather is hot. Deep grass can also hide all manner of nasties ready to crack differentials and sumps. If you have a catalytic converter fitted, it's quite possible for the red hot cat to set the grass alight when you stop. Set fire to some grass on a green lane and

Driving across areas of grass makes for a satisfying day out, but be wary of hidden obstacles.

burn down a farmer's crop of nice ripe wheat or barley and you won't be popular.

Under certain conditions, lush wet grass can be like an ice rink. Of course, with mud terrain tyres this shouldn't be much of a problem, but beware on side slopes.

Rocks

My experience of driving rocks is fairly limited, but it is particularly interesting from a technical point of view. Picking the best way through a seemingly impassable jumble of stones can be particularly gratifying. Beware, though; of all the disciplines we've looked at rocks are the least forgiving. One little slip can cause huge amounts of damage. Nerf bars, a rollcage, and underbody protection are imperative

if you want to remain mobile. Ensure they are strong, well attached, and in the case of side bars, fairly flush fitting so they don't get caught up and limit ground clearance, but not so flush that they wreck your sills if you bend them. Other than that the usual rules apply. Slow, low gear and be careful. Oh, and if you're tempted to try and get more traction by lowering your tyre pressures, don't forget you will also reduce your ground clearance and your tyres will be far more susceptible to sidewall damage.

Thumbs

You must keep your thumbs out of the centre of the steering wheel. Catch your wheel in a rut, at even low speed, and the steering wheel will spin wildly, and the spoke of the wheel will catch your thumb faster than you can react. Catch a thumb in one of the holes in a nice aftermarket steering wheel and, well, I'll leave the rest to your imagination.

Chapter 8
Special vehicles

This chapter is specifically designed to show you what can be achieved and inspire you to develop your truck into something out of the ordinary. There are now thousands of Suzuki 4x4s around the world that are unlike anything the designers at Suzuki intended.

These range from body swap kits, to huge V8 monster trucks and the Pike's Peak winning 1000bhp Escudos (Grand Vitara), all at least loosely based on Suzukis in some shape or form. Whilst you may not wish to emulate these extreme machines, certain elements of their style and minor modifications can be utilised in your own vehicle. And, let's face it, if nothing else they are certainly nice to look at!

I've also included a couple of the better known body replacement kits here, as they can be an economical alternative to scrapping a truck with a rusting shell but good

There might not be much Suzuki in it, but you've got to admit, you want one, don't you?
(Courtesy Spidertrax)

chassis and mechanicals, and make excellent base vehicles for further modification.

BLITZ

This is one very classy-looking off-road buggy kit. Developed by Blitz Midland over several years, these reasonably-priced, off the

shelf, bolt-on kits are now a fairly common sight at off-road events in the UK, and acquit themselves very well.

The kits comprise a 48mm BS1387 Medium Weight Blue Band Tube space frame body replacement, with a similar detachable front end giving excellent engine access, and

The SJ-based Blitz is a great-looking shell replacement kit.
(Courtesy Blitz Midland)

The soft-top and spare wheel carrier are optional extras.
(Courtesy Blitz Midland)

a new bonnet. It's obviously far easier to fit much needed additions, such as a snorkel, during the build, but with so much bodywork having been dispensed with, it's a far simpler prospect to undertake further modifications than on a standard truck. Various other accessories, such as a rear spare wheel mounting bracket and three-piece soft-top roof are also available direct from the manufacturer.

Apart from the new components, the kit uses most of

the parts from the original donor vehicle. The complete chassis and running gear, the suspension, transmission, petrol tank, exhaust, radiator, seats, belts, pedals, lights (except headlights) and even the hinges and bonnet catch are all retained, making conversion not only a quick and easy process, but a relatively economical one as well. In fact, all that is necessary to get the vehicle roadworthy are the windscreen, and a pair of plastic truck wheelarches. As the original chassis is retained unaltered, the new vehicle is exempt from Single Vehicle Approval in the UK, a simple change to the vehicle's body type on the logbook being all that is required.

Off-road the benefits are immediately obvious. The loss of a large amount of weight means that performance is significantly improved. Not only is the power to weight ratio increased, but the Suzuki's ability to float over obstacles is further enhanced. The approach and departure angles are virtually non-existent, and the ground clearance is also increased.

The Blitz conversion has to be a serious consideration for a rotten-bodied truck with good running gear. (Courtesy Blitz Midland)

These, together with the possibility of fitting virtually any tyre size you like, with some minor adjustments during construction, makes the Blitz a very attractive proposition off-road.

In fact, it would probably be no exaggeration to say that, with rusty donor vehicles readily available for little outlay, the entire kit and the original vehicle can be had for about the same cost as a late model, good condition Samurai, the only difference being that a Blitz has significantly better off-road ability than a standard truck and would be considerably simpler to modify.

KAP BANDIT
The KAP Bandit has been around since 2002 and has been steadily developing since then up to the latest 3.5-litre, V6 Cosworth-engined version. It would be fair to say that, other than shape, it has little to do with a Suzuki, Jimny or otherwise. However, it has the spirit of a Suzuki, and that's good enough for me.

The chassis is a complete tubular steel space frame with an aluminium engine compartment bulkhead, and additional flat and box section crossmembers for gearbox and engine mounting. The shell

Want a slightly different Jimny, how about a KAP bandit?

The Fox dampers allow a total of 14in of travel: 8in up and 6in down.

The KAP Bandit at play.
(Courtesy KAP Suzuki)

Glass fibre panels, moulded from a Jimny, surround the spaceframe chassis.

The 3.5-litre V6 Ford Cosworth engine gives 312bhp at the wheels.

The radiator is presently front-mounted but will soon be out of harm's way at the rear.

A four-speed Quaife sequential dog box and a Trevor Milner 1.75:1 ratio transfer box transfer the power to the Land Rover 90 V8 axles.

is GRP, as are the doors, bonnet and engine cowl. The occupants are safely ensconced in a pair of Corbeau seats, and strapped in with Luke four-point race harnesses.

A World Rally Car pedal box ensures everything is okay in the foot control department. The brake system boasts twin brake master cylinders, just in case you should manage to rip out a brake pipe on your travels, and braided hoses connect this to the four Cosworth brake callipers, so there should be no problem stopping.

The engine has gone from a 2.0-litre Vauxhall, through the 2.9 V6 Cosworth from a Ford Granada Scorpio, to the latest 3.5-litre version of the same engine giving 312bhp at the wheels. For a vehicle that only weighs in at 1127kg, that's a pretty serious power to weight ratio. Cooling all that power is a custom-made aluminium radiator, front-mounted at present, but plans are in the pipeline to have it rear-mounted to reduce the risk of damage and mud blocking the core.

The engine is connected to a four-speed Quaife sequential dog box, which runs through a Trevor Milner 1.75:1 ratio transfer box, on its way to the Land Rover 90 V8 axles. If any stock axle is likely to take the abuse the screaming Cosworth power unit will throw at it then this is the one. Drilled front radius arms, modified to take Td5 Land Rover bushes, keep these in place, whilst heavy-duty, rose-jointed panhard rods ensure there is no sideways movement. All the props are custom-built, with one or two running close to their angular limit, although they seem to bear no ill effect for all that.

Spring over Fox remote reservoir dampers look after the suspension. A bit of overkill on what is supposedly a Comp Safari machine, but it's likely that it will see some hill rally events during its life. The Fox system gives a total of 14in of travel, 8in up and 6in down.

The petrol tank is a custom-built, wedge-shaped, foam-filled aluminium job, and kept well away from danger behind a substantial amount of the space frame chassis. The tank is connected to the engine via high spec braided hoses. The air intake is protected by a massive K&N cone filter and is well out of the way of any water or foreign bodies.

A large, quick-ratio, power-assisted steering box is linked to one of the few pieces of original Jimny surviving, the steering column. This is located in the stock

The replacement Scamp body bolts straight onto the original chassis mounting points. (Courtesy Scamp Motor Company)

The Rowfant might raise a few eyebrows off-road. (Courtesy Scamp Motor Company)

(almost) dashboard, which joins the door handles in completing the list of Suzuki parts. The next stage in development will be to make the Bandit road legal.

SCAMP MOTOR COMPANY

The Scamp Motor Company came into existence in 1969 when BMC axed the Mini Moke. The Mini-based Mk 1 Scamp continued in production until 1977 when a new chassis was developed. In 1987, ownership of the Scamp Motor Company passed to its current owner Andrew MacLean, who immediately set about updating the design.

Early 1996 saw the start of the interesting bit as far as Suzuki owners are concerned, with the change from Mini to 4x4 base vehicles, with the introduction of the next 4x4. The GT4x4 was the first prototype: the styling was later amended from that of the GT of 1993 to the more practical door aperture of the Mk 3. The company's concentration on the four-wheel drive models, together with the requirements of SVA Regulations, lead to the withdrawal of Mini based kits at the end of 1999.

The replacement Scamp body is bolted straight onto the original mounting points, which are employed for accurate and safe assembly. It's only necessary for the builder to examine the mechanical components, fuel and brake lines of the donor vehicle, and paint, trim and wire the new body to complete the new vehicle. If a good quality donor is chosen, the running gear can be left untouched, which makes for a quick and easy transformation.

In 2000 the Rowfant was born. Based on an SJ chassis and similar in principle to the Scamp its classic car lines should certainly raise a few eyebrows at your local off-road site.

SPIDERTRAX M2G

Not content with modifying stock Suzuki 4x4s, Spidertrax produced a prototype recreational buggy. This

All Spidertrax kit is developed on the trail. (Courtesy Spidertrax)

The M2G from Spidertrax looks like it might be fun! (Courtesy Spidertrax)

If the kit performs like this here, think what it will do to your Samurai.
(Courtesy Spidertrax)

space framed beauty owes much of its lineage to off-road racing machines but has been developed with fun in mind. The engine is mid-mounted, and the two-seat configuration offers excellent all-round visibility and low centre of gravity. As you might expect, axle articulation is excellent.

Additionally, whilst developing the M2G several innovations to the running gear have been achieved. A new twin stick transfer box has been built that allows 2-wheel drive (rear output only) or 4-wheel drive to be selected on one lever, and Low or High on the other. This is combined with Spider 9 Axles, which utilise a 9in third member with chromoly axle shaft options with up to 40 splines. This 9in third member is made extremely versatile by its almost endless configuration options, such as steel or aluminium third members, ring and pinion gear ratios as low as 6.5, and just about any type of locker imaginable. It also boasts an octagonal centre similar in design to Spidertrax's own Sidewinder Axles. Using 3in x ¼in wall axle tubes and box construction trussing means it is extremely strong, whilst still retaining a very low weight.

At the ends of the front axles are the new Lightweight 60 Knuckles. Laser cut, they are just the ticket for real off-road performance. They are significantly smaller, lighter, and more durable than other knuckles on the market, and with a ball and race mounting system using two ¾in bolts for assembling the knuckles, serviceability is as easy as removing two bolts. These new ends work with any axle using Dana type 60 u-joints.

As you can see in the photographs, this is a superb machine, with huge amounts of articulation, balance and overall ability. It is the ultimate Suzuki fun off-road modification and I for one, want one!

V6 AND V8 ENGINE SWAPS

There is a firm in Tampa, Florida that does V6 and V8 Samurai conversions. Alan Kempton's Suzuki Lightning Conversions can build you a 4.3 V6 Chevy Vortec, a 318 V8 Chevy or even a 350cid V8 Chevy Corvette-engined Samurai. Or, if you fancy having a go yourself, the company also offers various V6 kits based on the 4.3 Chevy Vortec engine.

The company started in 1986, fitting V8s to two-wheel drive Samurais, and the installations look superb. The company also offers

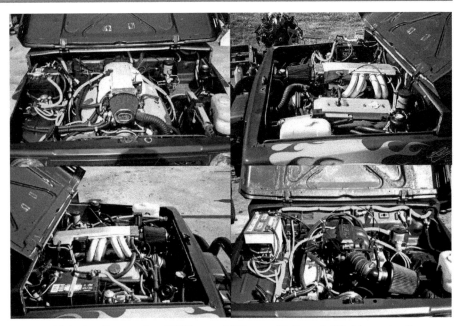

Lightning Conversions' V8 Samurai. Who wouldn't want 400+bhp on tap? (Courtesy Lightning Conversions)

Whether V6 or V8, the transplant looks superb. (Courtesy Lightning Conversions)

a V6 conversion for the Vitara, so there's no need to feel left out if you run a coiler. Of course, it's possible to do these conversions yourself, but it's much easier when someone else has done all the hard work for you.

A Range Rover-chassised SJ might not be for purists, but it certainly has some appeal. (Courtesy Steve Abbott)

the photographs was found by its present owner languishing in a field, with most of its interior and ancillaries stripped out. The shortened Range Rover chassis obviously makes for a much superior ramp breakover angle, combine this with Pro Comp springs and dampers and you have something of a beast. The Rover 3.5-litre V8 engine has benefited from a Weber twin choke carburettor with anti-dump jets, and the exhaust is taken care of by a set of Hedman headers and a straight through system.

The transmission sports air lockers and a low ratio transfer box, which should keep it going through

You have to look pretty close to tell it's not really a Suzuki. (Courtesy Steve Abbott)

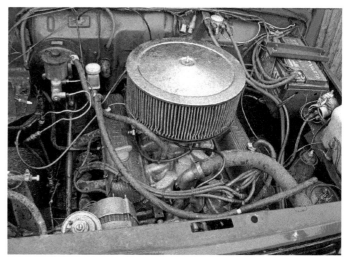

There aren't that many 3.5-litre V8 SJs about, which makes them a bit special. (Courtesy Steve Abbott)

V8 RANGE ROVER/SJ HYBRID

It is possible, as mentioned previously, to fit almost any engine into any vehicle so long as it is physically capable of accommodating it, and there are many examples around the world of V6 and V8 engines having been squeezed into Suzukis. However (all you Suzuki purists look away) there is another way. The 3.5-litre V8 Range Rover is a pretty capable beast off-road, and bob-tailed, with modified suspension, you would have to admit it's pretty damn good. It follows then that if you could cut the chassis down a bit so it would sit under an SJ body shell, with all the loss of weight that would entail, you could expect a fairly capable machine.

So, what if you managed to find such a beast and then set about making it better? The machine in most things, and if not there is a 9000lb winch up front that will. The occupants aren't forgotten, as they are cosseted in some Volvo seats and, if the worst should happen, there is a full internal/external rollcage. Apart from all that it looks pretty spectacular too, and although not purely a Suzuki, it's a worthy addition to the family.

Appendix A
Glossary

Anti-roll bar
This is a torsion bar held on the front chassis members, with levers attached to either end of the axle or suspension links, that limits the differential travel of the wheels, thus reducing a vehicle's tendency to roll during cornering. It severely limits the suspension travel, though, and is, therefore, often the first thing to be ditched during modification for off-roading.

Approach angle
The angle between the front of the front wheel were it contacts the ground on a flat surface and the first obstacle encountered on the front of the vehicle. The greater the angle the better. This is often overlooked and can seriously detract from a vehicle's off-road ability.

Articulation
Articulation is the ability of the axles to move relative to the vehicle and each other, and thus the vehicle's ability to cover rough terrain. There are various meaningless measures relating to articulation. The only fair way to compare different vehicles is to use Ramp travel index. (See below)

Automatic choke
Most auto-chokes are, in fact, semi-automatic. Most are dependant on a wax pellet that expands and contracts with the engine temperature to drive an array of pushrods, levers and cogs that adjust the choke flap and tickover speed. Normally these are fine, but once they start to get a bit long in the tooth they can become a serious pain. For the sake of a small outlay and your sanity, at the first sign of problems chuck it and get a manual choke conversion.

Branch deflectors
Thin wire cables fixed taut between the top of the windscreen pillar and the front of the wing to deflect vegetation from striking the glass.

Bump steer
Hit a bump or pothole and the steering swings violently from side to side before depositing you in a ditch; this is bump steer. This is the result of the two steering rods, which should be kept parallel, being put at an increased angle to one another. Changing virtually any suspension component to gain lift will cause this. A drop Pitman arm or Z Bar steering rod will cure the situation. Fitting a steering damper will limit the symptoms but won't tackle the cause.

Carburettor
Basically, a carburettor is just a tube with a narrowing (a venturi)

that makes the air sucked through it accelerate through the narrowed section, thus lowering the pressure. This subsequently sucks atomised fuel from the jet placed in this low pressure area. Different circumstances and conditions require different air/fuel ratios and volumes, hence the complexity of a modern carburettor, which is trying to cope with conditions from 600-6000 revs and air temperatures as diverse as minus 5 to plus 30 degrees Celsius.

This requires a few additions to your simple tube. Firstly, you need something to allow you to enrich the fuel mixture to overcome cold starting conditions. This is commonly known as a choke and usually operates by restricting the amount of air flowing into the inlet. This is combined with a lever that raises the tickover slightly whilst the engine warms up. Modern vehicles will have a semi-automatic choke mechanism or, more likely, fuel injection.

If decent low and top end performance are to be achieved then, as it's not possible to cram enough air through the original pipe, a secondary choke is necessary. Basically similar to the first pipe, it doesn't need to have any of the starting mechanism on it as this is already dealt with in the first choke. The secondary choke just cuts-in to supplement the first choke under acceleration.

On initial acceleration there is a momentary hesitation when the huge rush of air flowing into the carb pre-empts the fuel flowing from the secondary choke. Unaided, the mixture becomes so weak the engine can't recover and stalls. A quick burst of fuel directly into the

choke stops this happening while the carb recovers. This little add-on is called the accelerator pump. Basically, on acceleration, it squirts a burst of fuel straight into the bore of the choke, which overcomes this temporary fuel starvation.

Caster angle
Vehicle steering has an inclined king pin to aid steering stability. An imaginary line drawn through the king pin would pass through the centre of the hub and would strike the ground a few centimetres in front of the centre of the point of contact of the tyre. This is positive caster, which not only ensures the wheel runs straight, but also assists the wheel in straightening after a turn.

Fitting long shackles, for instance, rotates the spring down at the front around the rear spring hanger, this changes the caster angle towards, and sometimes through, neutral caster and into negative caster. This is inherently dangerous and one of the reasons home-made Spring over axle conversions can be so deadly.

Catalytic converter
Most modern fuel injected (and even some late carburettored) vehicles will have a 'cat' fitted. You should ensure that the cat is protected as much as possible from damage off-road by fitting skid plates, if possible, and be aware that cats run very hot and after a good run during the summer months. If you park over long dry grass, the cat will give off sufficient heat to cause the vegetation to combust. You can rapidly lose your vehicle and, if in a farm setting, you run the risk of destroying valuable fields of crops.

Coil springs
Coils give far better ride and handling characteristics, although they can limit suspension travel and require a range of rods, etc., to locate the axle. Other than longer springs or spring packers, suspension modifications are expensive. However, if you're prepared to redesign the suspension completely, huge amounts of articulation can be achieved.

Constant velocity joints
CV joints as they are more commonly known are a complex form of universal joint. Normally they comprise an inner shaft fitted with a set of ball bearings in a cage, and mounted in elliptical grooves. The outer shaft has a grooved cup that fits over the bearing cage, the balls secured in straight grooves cut in the plane of the shaft. This enables the speed of both input and output shafts to remain equal regardless of the shafts' relative positions, up to their maximum operating angle (usually about 25 degrees).

Cross-axled
If you're traversing deeply rutted terrain you can occasionally find your diagonally opposite wheels leaving the ground simultaneously. This is cross-axling. If your vehicle isn't fitted with some form of differential lock then all power will be transmitted to the two free spinning wheels and motion will cease.

Departure angle
The angle between the back of the rear wheel were it is in contact with the ground on a flat surface, and the first part of the rear of the vehicle. This can seriously hinder a vehicle's

exit from an obstacle, and is even more likely to be overlooked than the approach angle.

Differential

A differential is used to transfer the drive from the engine/gearbox to the half shafts that are connected to the wheels. It also allows the outer wheel on a bend to rotate faster to cover the extra distance relative to the greater radius of the arc traversed by the wheel. This is achieved by using caged planetary gears that allow the half shafts to turn independently. The downside of this mechanism is that if one wheel loses traction all power is transferred to that wheel and locomotion is lost. (See differential lockers).

Differential lockers

There are three main ways of locking a differential. The first is the clutch type, such as the Detroit Locker, which acts like a permanently locked differential except that under excessive force a dog clutch can overcome its retaining springs and allow the differential mechanism to move one set of teeth across, rather like an automatic ratchet mechanism. This type of locker can be a great help off-road but can also significantly affect the on-road handling.

The second type is the manually operated locker, such as the Air Locker. At the touch of a button inside the cab the diff can be locked whilst on difficult terrain and released for on-road use.

The third way is to permanently weld the internal components of the differential. This can only be used for strictly off-road vehicles or catastrophic transmission failure will eventually occur.

D-shackles

A semicircular steel connector with a screw-in pin, used to secure winch and recovery ropes safely. Only those with a load testing should be used under the extreme forces experienced during vehicle recovery.

Farm jack or high-lift jack

A 70 year old design that consists of a holed steel tower with a climbing mechanism that lifts the vehicle. Available in different lengths up to several feet, care should be taken during use, as they can be very unstable at their upper limits, although this trait can also be infinitely useful if employed correctly.

Fire extinguisher

Obvious what it is, but do not venture off road without one. The mixture of unstable terrain, sources of ignition and flammable liquids can make for disaster.

Freewheeling hubs

A mechanism, either manual or automatic, fitted to the outer front hubs that allows the hub and wheel to be disconnected from the axle half shaft whilst in two-wheel drive; thus stopping the front half shafts, differential and prop shaft from rotating, creating better economy through not driving unnecessary components and reducing component wear.

Hangers

These are the chassis mounts that hang down from the chassis rails and hold the pivot end of a leaf spring.

Leaf springs

Laminated or parabolic semi-elliptic leaf springs are descended from cart springs, although their design and manufacture has improved considerably. They are, however, a simple, easily-modified form of suspension that positively locates the axles.

Panhard rod

Transverse stabiliser bar, on coil sprung suspension setups that connects the axle to the vehicle chassis to prevent sideways movement under load. More commonly found on race cars, these are now becoming more popular on modified off-road trucks.

Power steering

A system that uses a pump, driven by an additional belt from the engine pulleys, that reduces the force necessary to turn the steering wheel. Later models have this system as standard, and it's possible to obtain kits to fit the system to earlier models.

Ramp breakover angle

The angle between the front and rear wheels and the underside of the vehicle, used as a measure of a vehicle's ability to cross a hump without grounding the underside. The lower the better, large tyres and a short wheelbase reduce the angle significantly.

Ramp travel index

A measure of a vehicle's ability to articulate decided by its ability to drive up a single ramp on one side of the vehicle and keep the remaining three tyres in contact with the ground. The length of travel up the ramp divided by the wheelbase of the vehicle gives the RTI. Initially, these ramps were set at 20 degrees but, due to more vehicles being designed to super-articulate and gaining perfect 1000 scores, this has generally been increased to 23 degrees.

Rollcage

Due to the nature of the terrain and the design of off-road vehicles, a roll over is always a possibility even in seemingly innocuous areas. A rollcage, whether a simple single hoop behind the seats or a full four-seat design, will stop the vehicle roof (and occupants) crumpling under the weight of the vehicle.

Sand ladder

Short lengths of steel sheet, usually holed for weight reduction, that can be used beneath the wheels of a stuck vehicle to aid traction for recovery, they can also be used for bridging small gaps and ridges.

Shackles

Steel plates that connect the moving end of leaf springs. These are usually separate plates, but sets of lengthened shackles can have a central bar, or tube, to aid stability. Shackles can be lengthened to raise the suspension to allow larger tyres to be fitted, though they should be no more than 4in longer than standard to avoid dangerous changes in steering geometry.

Shackle reversal

A modification to the front leaf sprung suspension that swaps the pivoting and moving ends of the spring, this increases ride comfort and handling performance, and raises the suspension at the same time.

Side bars

Strong steel tubes, fixed directly to the chassis, that take impact from off-road obstructions, such as rocks and tree stumps, thus preventing damage to sill panels and door bottoms.

Side steps

Unnecessary fashion accessories akin to running boards on vintage cars. They severely limit ramp breakover angle and ground clearance. Not to be confused with side bars.

Skid plates

Heavy steel sheets fitted to vulnerable underbody components, such as the engine sump, gear and transfer boxes, axles and steering components, to prevent damage off-road.

Snatch block

Basically a pulley used during winching to increase the mechanical advantage or to enable a winch to be deployed at angles to a direct pull in unfavourable locations.

Snorkel

The raised air intake that allows a vehicle to be driven in deep water without the danger of taking water into the engine.

Steering damper

Works in the same manner as a suspension damper but fits between the chassis and the steering rods to damp out steering vibration. Can be wrongly used to conceal the detrimental effects of incorrectly-modified suspension systems.

Toe in

The front wheels on virtually all road-going vehicles are not parallel. They are usually adjusted 'toe in' which means that the fronts of the tyres are closer together than the rear, giving a pigeon toed appearance. This keeps the wheels rolling in a parallel direction and ensures the vehicle tracks straight on the highway. If the vehicle feels unstable and irregular tyre wear patterns are encountered, it's likely the tracking needs adjustment. It's possible to check toe in on your drive by simply measuring the distance between the tyre centres front and back of the front wheel and comparing lengths. The difference, assuming the front is shorter, is the amount of toe in. It's best to take teh vehicle to a garage and have it checked accurately.

Towing points

Towing points are essential if you are going off-road. They should be either welded to, or bolted securely through, the main chassis rails, and under no circumstances should vehicle transportation securing rings be used for towing.

Trailing arms

Suspension arms that locate the axle on a coil sprung live axle suspension setup, being bolted to the axle and chassis on either side. They can also help prevent rotation of the axle tube under load.

Transfer box

Any serious off-road vehicle will have a transfer box. This usually contains two or more sets of gears that allow the gearing to be lowered to enable high torque and low speeds to be used in difficult terrain. It can also enable the front transmission to be disconnected to allow the vehicle to run in rear-wheel drive only for road use. If no centre differential is fitted and two-wheel drive is not selected, transmission wind up will occur due to the differing relative speeds of opposite wheels whilst traversing bends.

Transmission brake

Older models have the handbrake fitted to the rear prop shaft, which effectively brakes all four wheels when in four-wheel drive. This can be advantageous in off-road conditions where rear wheel only braking might allow the vehicle to slip.

Universal joints

UJs allow drive to be transmitted through a variable angle in a shaft. Some simple forms are made with a rubber coupling, or doughnut, clamped between two yokes, the shaft's differential movement being taken up by the elasticity of the rubber.

On a 4x4, however, the most likely type you will find is the Hardy Spicer joint. This consists of a cruciform coupling that fits into cup bearings on the two twin yokes on the shaft ends, enabling the shafts to rotate whilst at an angle to one another. You will find UJs in the multitude of prop shafts in the vehicle transmission.

Waffles

A type of sand ladder, similar in appearance to the food item, placed beneath wheels to enable extraction when wheels are dug in. Can also be used for bridging small gaps and ridges.

Wheelbase

The wheelbase is the distance between the axle centres. The shorter the wheelbase the less ramp breakover angle and more manoeuvrability your vehicle will have, thus allowing for better off-road performance.

Appendix B
Useful contacts

MODIFIED KIT SUPPLIERS

4x4x4
UK supplier of a host of accessories, especially good for wheel and tyre combination deals. www.4x4x4.com

ARB 4x4
Australia's largest manufacturer and distributor of 4x4 accessories. With an office in the US and an export network that extends through more than 80 countries, ARB's air lockers are particularly worthy of note. www.arb.com.au

Badlands
About 700 acres in Attica, western Indiana, owned and operated by the Myers family. Not only a fantastic off-road site, but the guys here have been know to produce some pretty awesome trucks as well. www.badlandsoffroad.com

Big Balls Off-road
Could only be an Australian company!
www.bigballsoffroad.com

Breeze Industries
Supplier of Suzuki off-road kit, based in Coquitlam, Vancouver, Canada. www.breezeindustries.com

Bronco Tyres
Manufacturer of off-road tyres in the UK. Has a reputation for supplying economical tyres with big performance, such as the awesome Grizzly Claw. www.bronco4x4.com

Calmini
Bakersfield, California-based manufacturer of Suzuki suspension and performance parts, and so much more. Calmini has become synonymous with Suzuki modifications during the last decade. www.pursesuzuki.com

DG Tuning
Tuning specialist; in particular gears, axles and engine/ignition adaptors. www.Dgtuning.com

Explorer UK
UK distributor for Explorer Competition Products Inc of San Diego, California; in particular, the world-renowned ProComp performance dampers. www.explorerprocomp.co.uk

HAWK Strictly Suzuki
Supplier of new and used parts, service kits and modified gear, from Merlin, Oregon. www.hawksuzukiparts.com

KAP Suzuki
Yorkshire-based specialist in building modified and competition spec Suzukis, especially Jimnys. Home of the Jimny Bandit Comp Safari machine. www.KAPsuzuki4x4.co.uk

LA Supertrux
Nigel Morris's Daventry UK company, supplies various pieces of Suzuki kit and undertakes serious modification work. Home of the UK 'Bigfoot' and Monster Truck Racing scene. www.Supertrux.com

Overland
Supplier of kit for various makes, including snorkels and bumpers. www.overlandcomponents.co.uk

Petroworks
Manufacturer and supplier of a huge range of off-road kit aimed at Suzukis. The on-line catalogue holds an awesome array of kit for you to drool over. www.petroworks.com

Rhino Central
Supplier of inexpensive, yet effective kit. Makes the D-Flex extending shackle. www.Rhinocentral.co.uk

Roadless Gear
Supplier of kit and accessories. Not all Suzuki but well worth a look. www.roadlessgear.com

Rock 4X Fabrication
A small company with some big ideas and great kit. Based in Kenosha, Wisconsin. www.rock4xfabrication.com

Rocky Road Outfitters
Glenn Wakefield's company, supplier of trick bits for various makes of 4x4. www.Rocky-road.com

Shrockworks
Another well known company with a great reputation. From Houston, Texas, Shrockworks specialises in under-body armour and bumpers, not just for Suzukis either. www.shrockworks.com

SKY Manufacturing
Manufacturer of Suzuki modified kit. From Springfield, Oregon. www.sky-manufacturing.com

Spidertrax
Eddie Casanueva and Tom Kingston's company based in Longmont, Colorado. Some of the best designed and produced kit you'll find anywhere. Building extreme off-road machines for a living and based in the Rockies, these guys must even smile in their sleep. www.spidertrax.com

Suzuki Lightning Conversions
Alan Kempton's company based in Tampa Florida. Specialises in fitting V6 and V8 Chevy engines into Samurais. There have got to be worse ways of earning a crust. www.suzukiconversion.com

Suzisport
Modified and standard kit suppliers from Queensland Australia. www.suzisport.com

Trail Tough Products
The company name says it all. More excellent modified Suzuki kit from this Medford, Oregon based firm. www.trailtough.com

Wheelers Off-road
Off-road kit supplier from Grants Pass, Oregon, with a good range of Suzuki off-road kit. www.wheelersoffroad.com

KIT CARS
Blitz Midland
Manufacturer of the SJ-based Blitz. www.Blitzmidlands.fsnet.co.uk

Scamp Motor Company
Manufacturer of the Scamp Mk 4x4 and Rowfant. www.scampmotorcompany.co.uk

CLUBS AND FORUMS
4x4 Web
Massive 4x4 resource site with links to a huge amount of information. Site includes 20 sub-sites. www.4x4web.co.uk

Difflock
Multi-marque site with a multitude of forums and a shop. www.Difflock.com

iZook
A great site for everything Suzuki. Based in the US but just as relevant anywhere. www.izook.com

LJ10
An absolute must visit site for anyone with an L series Suzuki. www.lj10.com

Mudmuppets
Suzuki club, worthy of inclusion if only for the name! www.freewebs.com/Mudmuppets

Norfolkrhinos
The author's own club for Suzuki off-roaders in East Anglia. www.Norfolkrhinos.co.uk

North Brisbane Suzuki 4x4 Club
Another Aussie Suzuki Club, great website. www.nbs4x4club.com

Offroad.com
A huge amount of off-road information, you owe it to yourself to visit this site. www.offroad.com/suzuki

Offroading.net
UK-based bulletin board and resource centre. www.offroading.net

Raging Rhinos
Kent and South East based Suzuki club. www.Raging-rhinos.co.uk

Rhinoriders
Southeast UK-based Suzuki club. www.rhinoridersclub.co.uk

Shropshire Suzuki Club
Shropshire Suzuki Club, run by the owner of the 'Generation-X' X-90. www.groups.msn.com/shropshiresuzuki

Suzuki 4-Wheel Drive Club of New South Wales
A four-wheel drive, camping and bush touring club based in Ermington, NSW. www.suzuki4wd.com.au

Suzuki Four-Wheel Drive Club of South Australia
http://suzukisa.txc.net.au

Suzuki Four-Wheel Drive Club of Western Australia
http//home.off-road.com/~suzukiwa

Suzuki Club UK
Independent National Club for Suzuki off-roaders. www.geocities.com/suzukiclubuk

Suzuki Rhino Club
Official Suzuki Club for the UK, has a quarterly magazine and offers driver training and family fun days. Also organises the annual Rhino Rally. www.suzukirhinoclub.co.uk

Suzuki-Samurai Netherlands
English version of the popular Dutch website. www.suzuki-samurai.nl/foto-index/hoofd-index-eng.html

Suzuki Storm
Midlands-based Suzuki club. www.Suzuki-storm.co.uk

ZookPower
Another club-based site but from Ontario, Canada, with some nice trick trucks. www.zookpower.ca

Zuki 4x4
Suzuki club in Warwickshire run by Tim Weston of Rhinocentral. www.groups.msn.com/zuki4x4

Zuks Un Ltd UK
Based in the south west, offers tips, photos, competitions, trucks for sale and a catalogue. Members of Club ZULU are entitled to purchase discounted price parts and accessories. www.Zuks-un-ltd-uk.freeservers.com

Zukiworld Online
Fantastic US e-zine resource dedicated to providing information on Suzukis. This one is a must see. www.zukiworld.com

More from Veloce ...

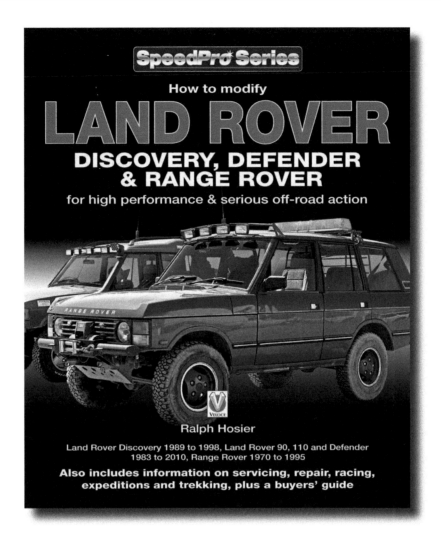

Buying a Range Rover, Land Rover Discovery or Defender can be just the start of a wonderful adventure. This book describes the options available to the owner, from big wheels and suspension lifts, under-body protection and tuning ideas, right up to how to convert the car into a high speed racer or an international expedition vehicle. With clear, jargon-free instructions, advice on events like family weekend green-laning, international expeditions and full-on competition, accompanied by colour photographs throughout, this is the definitive guide to getting the most from these exciting vehicles.

ISBN: 978-1-845843-15-1
Paperback • 25x20.7cm • 128 pages • 312 colour pictures

For more information and price details, visit our website at
www.veloce.co.uk
email: info@veloce.co.uk • Tel: +44(0)1305 260068

How to choose the right camshaft or camshafts for your individual application. Takes the mystery out of camshaft timing and tells you how to obtain optimum timing for maximum power. Applies to all four-stroke car-type engines.

ISBN: 978-1-903706-59-6
Paperback • 25x20.7cm • 64 pages • 95 colour and b&w pictures

For more information and price details, visit our website at
www.veloce.co.uk
email: info@veloce.co.uk • Tel: +44(0)1305 260068

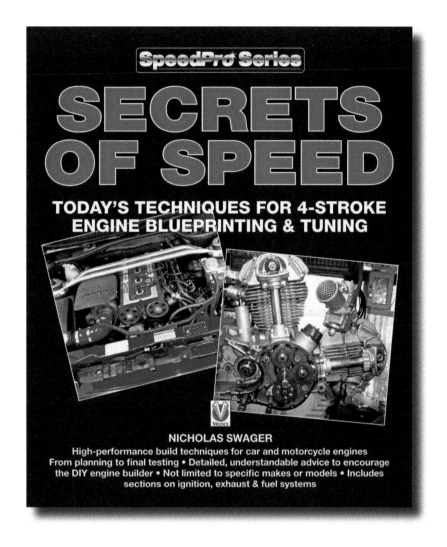

The process of building 4-stroke engines to a professional standard, from selecting materials and planning work, right through to methods of final assembly and testing, written for the DIY engine builder in an easy-to-understand style, and supported by approximately 200 photographs and original drawings. Containing five engine inspection and build sheets, and the contact details of approximately 45 specialist manufacturers and motorsport suppliers, the book explains build methods common to all 4-stroke engines, rather than specific makes or models. An essential purchase for all engine-building enthusiasts.

ISBN: 978-1-845842-97-0
Paperback • 25x20.7cm • 128 pages • 201 colour and b&w pictures

For more information and price details, visit our website at
www.veloce.co.uk
email: info@veloce.co.uk • Tel: +44(0)1305 260068

Simple, cost-effective, basic and reliable tips to ensure that any rally car stands a chance of reaching the finishing line. If you are planning a road-based rally, don't even think of leaving home before reading this book and implementing the tried and tested mods it describes so well.

ISBN: 978-1-845842-08-6
Paperback • 25x20.7cm • 96 pages • 154 colour and b&w pictures

For more information and price details, visit our website at
www.veloce.co.uk
email: info@veloce.co.uk • Tel: +44(0)1305 260068

Index